THOMAS JEFFERSON
GREAT AMERICAN

by Matt Doeden
illustrated by Gordon Purcell and
Terry Beatty

Capstone press

Mankato, Minnesota

Graphic Library is published by Capstone Press,
151 Good Counsel Drive, P.O. Box 669, Mankato, Minnesota 56002.
www.capstonepress.com

Printed in the United States of America

1 2 3 4 5 6 11 10 09 08 07 06

Library of Congress Cataloging-in-Publication Data
Doeden, Matt.
Thomas Jefferson: great American / by Matt Doeden; illustrated by Gordon Purcell and Terry Beatty.
p. cm.—(Graphic library. Graphic biographies)
Summary: "In graphic novel format, tells the life story of President Thomas Jefferson, who authored the Declaration of Independence"—Provided by publisher.
Includes bibliographical references and index.
ISBN-13: 978-0-7368-5488-7 (hardcover)
ISBN-10: 0-7368-5488-6 (hardcover)
ISBN-13: 978-0-7368-6887-7 (softcover pbk.)
ISBN-10: 0-7368-6887-9 (softcover pbk.)
1. Jefferson, Thomas, 1743–1826—Juvenile literature. 2. Presidents—United States—Biography—Juvenile literature. I. Purcell, Gordon, ill. II. Beatty, Terry, ill. III. Title. IV. Series.
E332.79.D64 2006
973.4'6092—dc22 2005031211

Art Direction
Bob Lentz

Designer
Jason Knudson

Storyboard Artist
Gordon Purcell

Production Designer
Alison Thiele

Colorist
Benjamin Hunzeker

Editor
Christine Peterson

pstone Press thanks Robin Gabriel, Hunter J. Smith Director of Education for the omas Jefferson Foundation, for her assistance with this book.

litor's note: Direct quotations from primary sources are indicated by a yellow background.

rect quotations appear on the following pages:
ge 8, Statement attributed to Jefferson in *A Winter in Washington* by Margaret Bayard Smith, (New York: 1824).
ge 13, from an 1822 letter written by John Adams (http://www.constitution.org/primarysources/pickering.html).
ge 14, from the Declaration of Independence as displayed at the National Archives in Washington, D.C. (http://www.archives.gov/national-archives-experience/charters/declaration_transcript.html).
ge 18, from a 1782 letter by Jefferson, (http://www.yale.edu/lawweb/avalon/jefflett/let19.htm).
ge 22, from Jefferson's first inaugural address, as published in *Jefferson the President: First Term, 1801-1805,* by Dumas Malone (Boston: Little, Brown, 1948).
Page 26, from a letter by Jefferson published in *The Writings of Thomas Jefferson*, (Washington, D.C., 1905).

TABLE OF CONTENTS

CHAPTER 1

Young Thomas Jefferson 4

CHAPTER 2

Family Man and
Founding Father 8

CHAPTER 3

Triumph and Tragedy 16

CHAPTER 4

President Jefferson 22

More about Thomas Jefferson..... 28
Glossary 30
Internet Sites 30
Read More 31
Bibliography................ 31
Index.................... 32

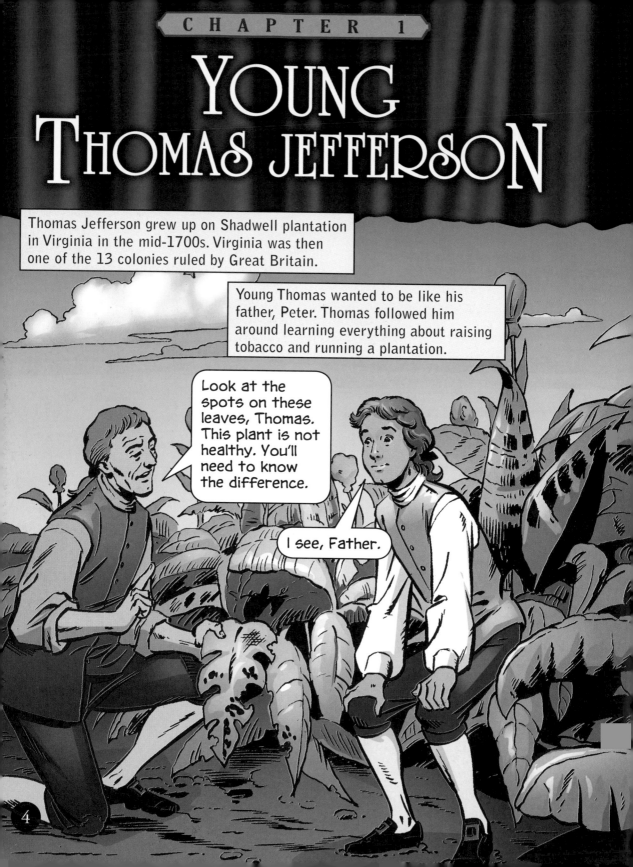

CHAPTER 1

YOUNG THOMAS JEFFERSON

Thomas Jefferson grew up on Shadwell plantation in Virginia in the mid-1700s. Virginia was then one of the 13 colonies ruled by Great Britain.

Young Thomas wanted to be like his father, Peter. Thomas followed him around learning everything about raising tobacco and running a plantation.

Look at the spots on these leaves, Thomas. This plant is not healthy. You'll need to know the difference.

I see, Father.

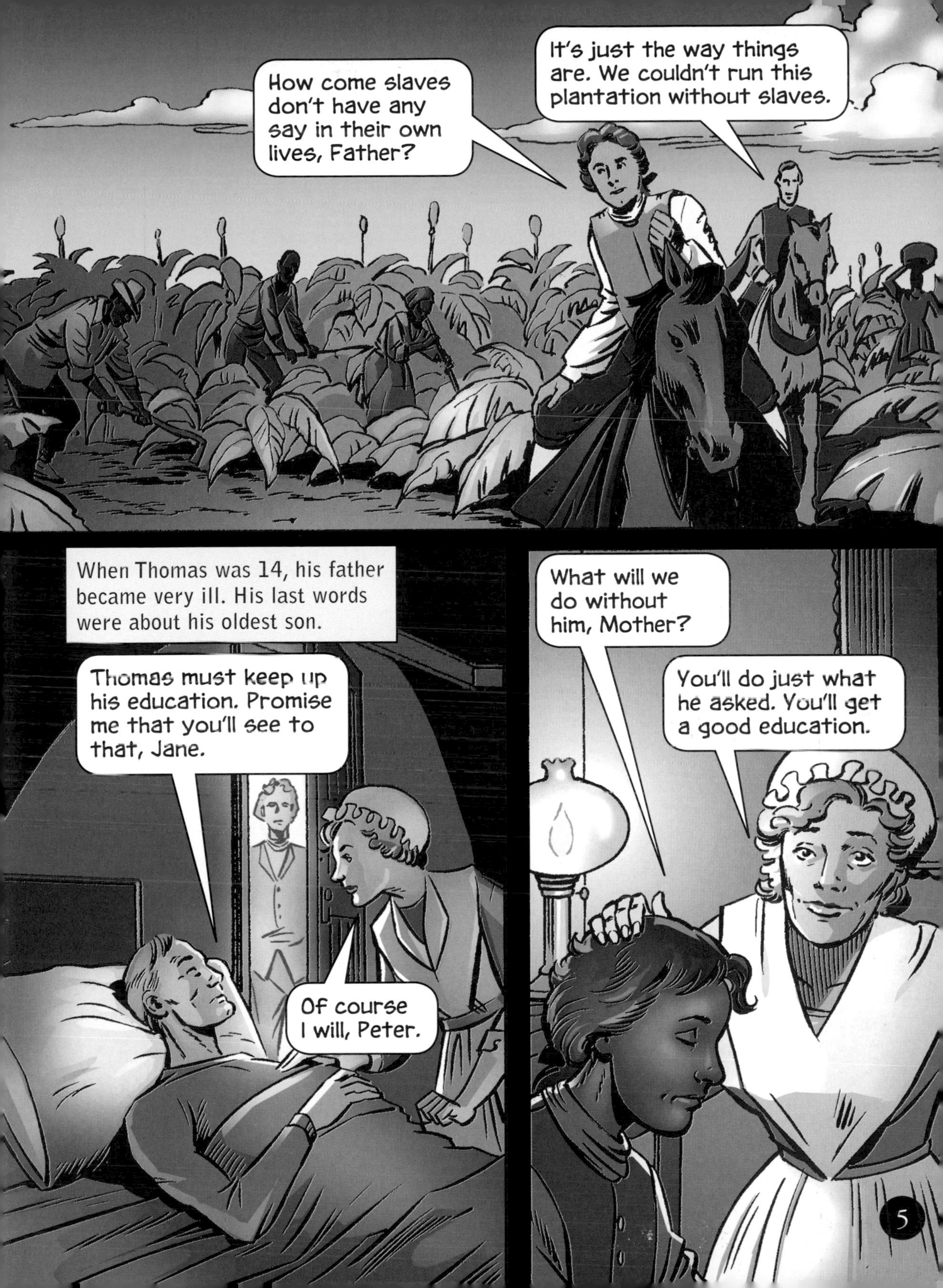
How come slaves don't have any say in their own lives, Father?
It's just the way things are. We couldn't run this plantation without slaves.
When Thomas was 14, his father became very ill. His last words were about his oldest son.
Thomas must keep up his education. Promise me that you'll see to that, Jane.
Of course I will, Peter.
What will we do without him, Mother?
You'll do just what he asked. You'll get a good education.

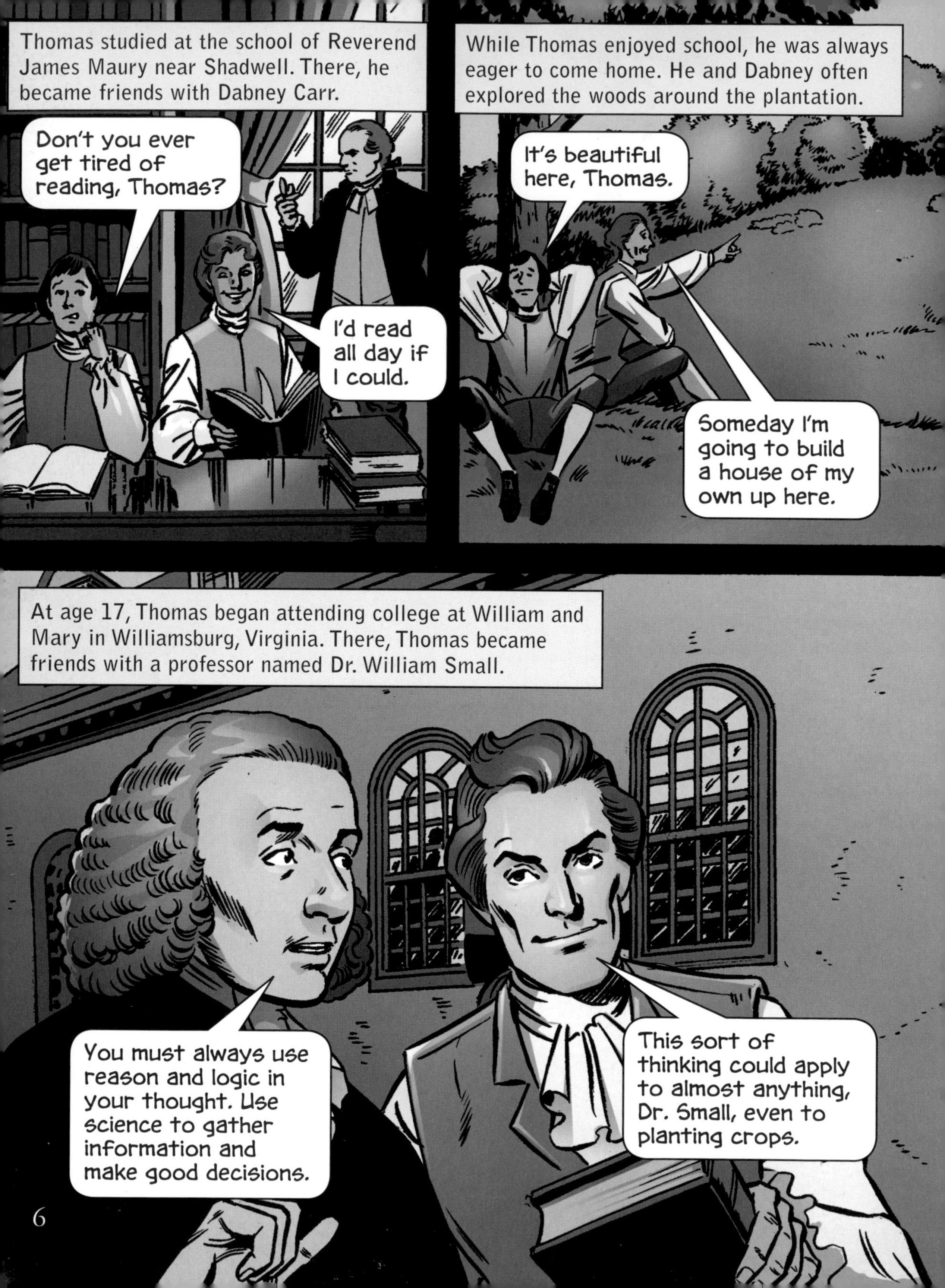
Thomas studied at the school of Reverend James Maury near Shadwell. There, he became friends with Dabney Carr.
Don't you ever get tired of reading, Thomas?
I'd read all day if I could.
While Thomas enjoyed school, he was always eager to come home. He and Dabney often explored the woods around the plantation.
It's beautiful here, Thomas.
Someday I'm going to build a house of my own up here.
At age 17, Thomas began attending college at William and Mary in Williamsburg, Virginia. There, Thomas became friends with a professor named Dr. William Small.
You must always use reason and logic in your thought. Use science to gather information and make good decisions.
This sort of thinking could apply to almost anything, Dr. Small, even to planting crops.

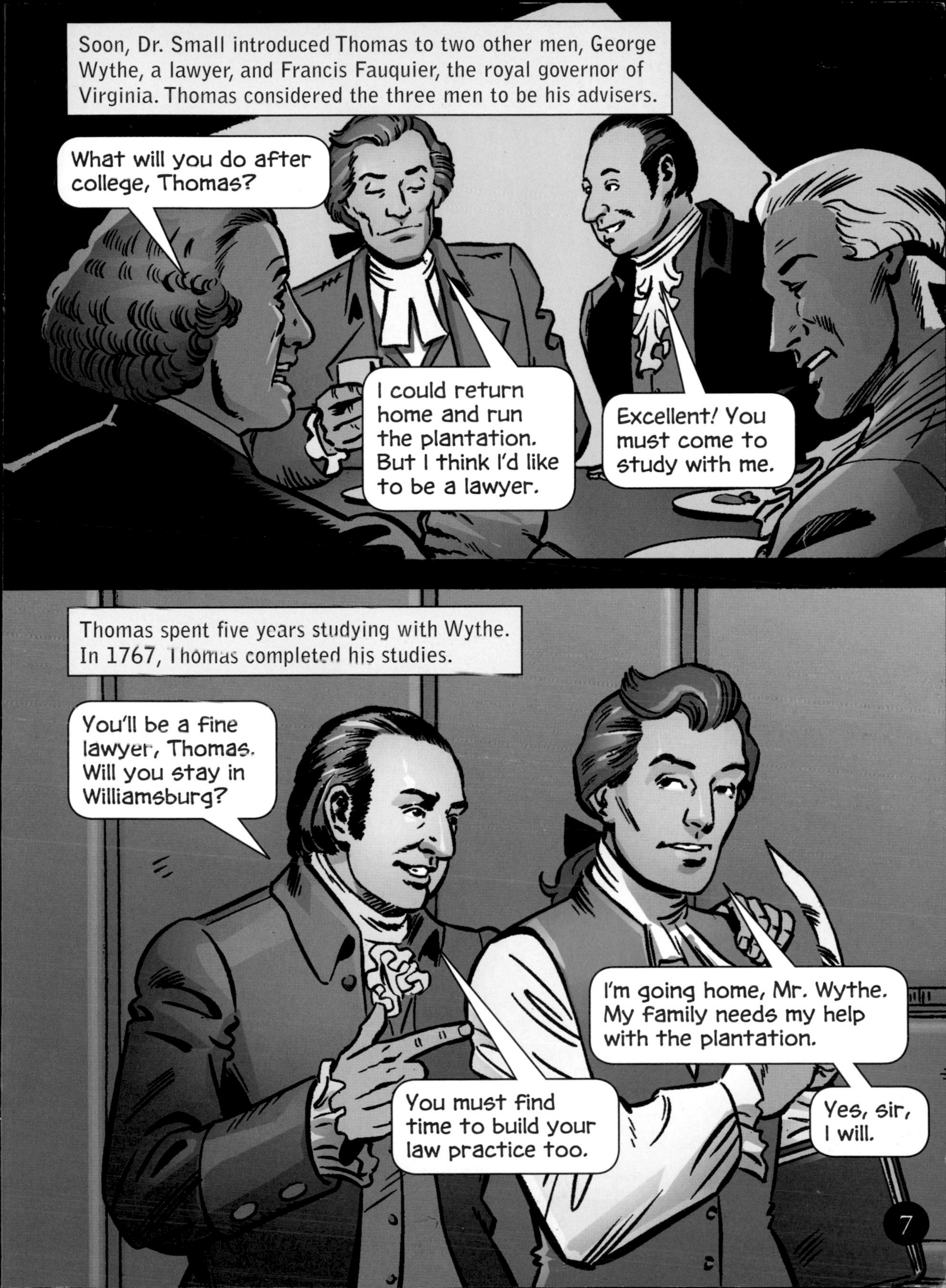
Soon, Dr. Small introduced Thomas to two other men, George Wythe, a lawyer, and Francis Fauquier, the royal governor of Virginia. Thomas considered the three men to be his advisers.
What will you do after college, Thomas?
I could return home and run the plantation. But I think I'd like to be a lawyer.
Excellent! You must come to study with me.
Thomas spent five years studying with Wythe. In 1767, Thomas completed his studies.
You'll be a fine lawyer, Thomas. Will you stay in Williamsburg?
I'm going home, Mr. Wythe. My family needs my help with the plantation.
You must find time to build your law practice too.
Yes, sir, I will.

CHAPTER 2

FAMILY MAN and FOUNDING FATHER

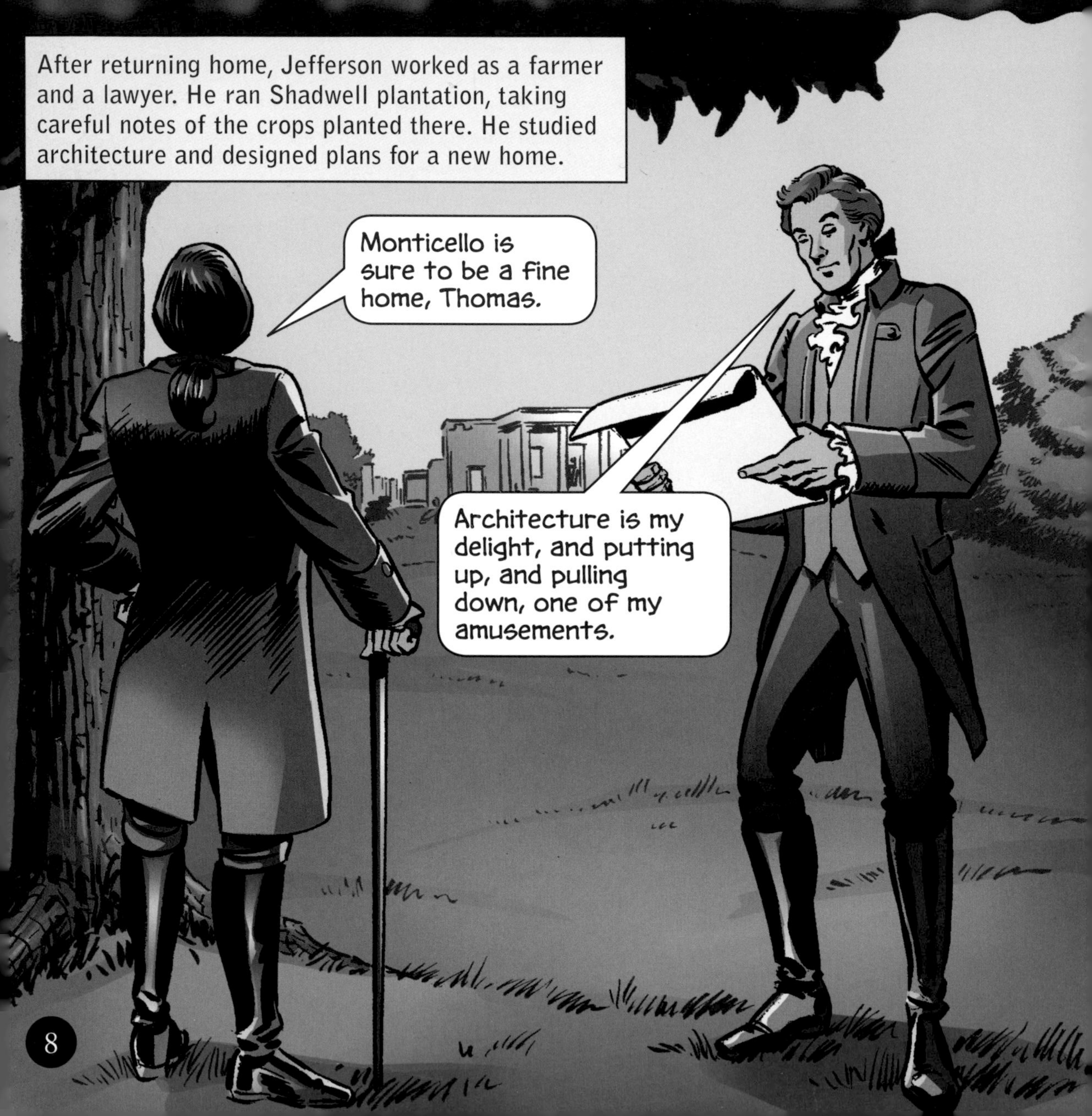
After returning home, Jefferson worked as a farmer and a lawyer. He ran Shadwell plantation, taking careful notes of the crops planted there. He studied architecture and designed plans for a new home.
Monticello is sure to be a fine home, Thomas.
Architecture is my delight, and putting up, and pulling down, one of my amusements.

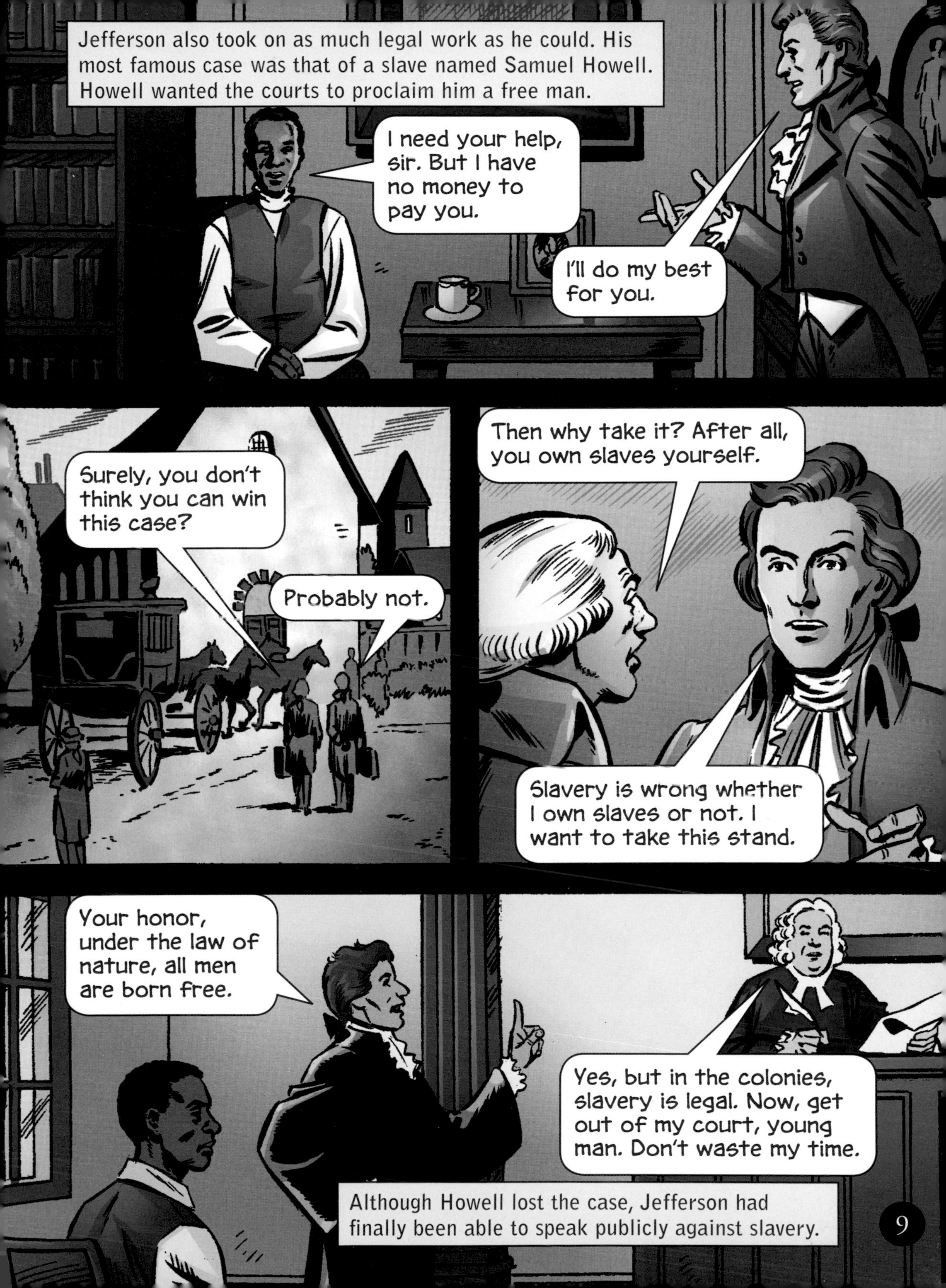

Jefferson also took on as much legal work as he could. His most famous case was that of a slave named Samuel Howell. Howell wanted the courts to proclaim him a free man.
I need your help, sir. But I have no money to pay you.
I'll do my best for you.
Surely, you don't think you can win this case?
Probably not.
Then why take it? After all, you own slaves yourself.
Slavery is wrong whether I own slaves or not. I want to take this stand.
Your honor, under the law of nature, all men are born free.
Yes, but in the colonies, slavery is legal. Now, get out of my court, young man. Don't waste my time.
Although Howell lost the case, Jefferson had finally been able to speak publicly against slavery.

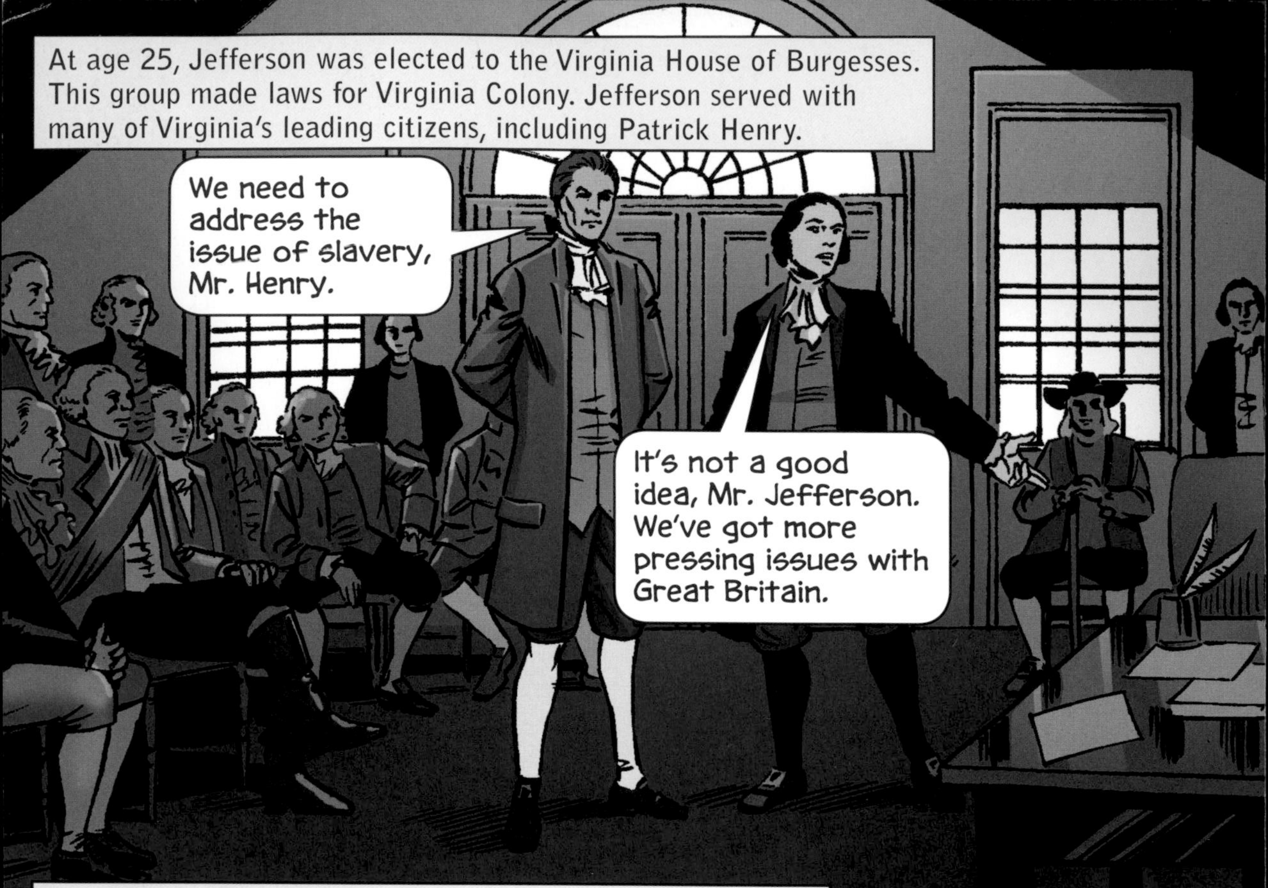
At age 25, Jefferson was elected to the Virginia House of Burgesses. This group made laws for Virginia Colony. Jefferson served with many of Virginia's leading citizens, including Patrick Henry.
We need to address the issue of slavery, Mr. Henry.
It's not a good idea, Mr. Jefferson. We've got more pressing issues with Great Britain.

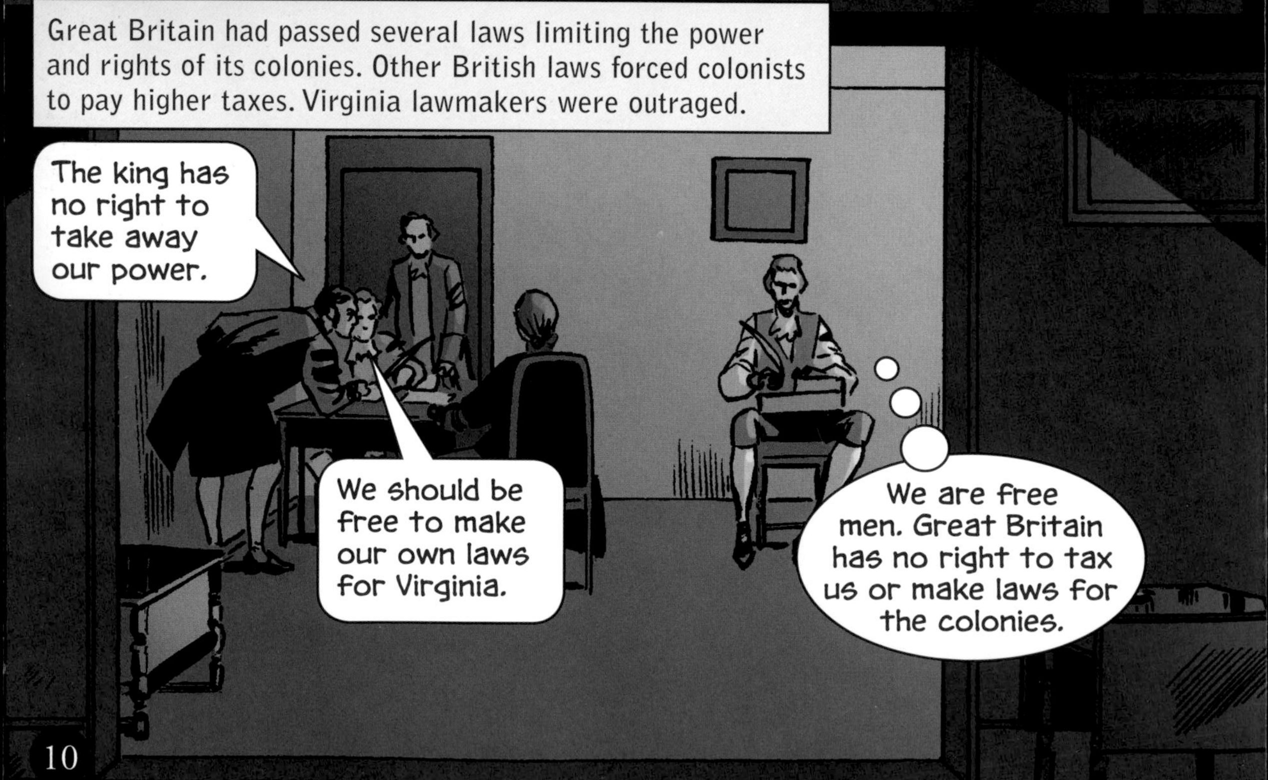
Great Britain had passed several laws limiting the power and rights of its colonies. Other British laws forced colonists to pay higher taxes. Virginia lawmakers were outraged.
The king has no right to take away our power.
We should be free to make our own laws for Virginia.
We are free men. Great Britain has no right to tax us or make laws for the colonies.

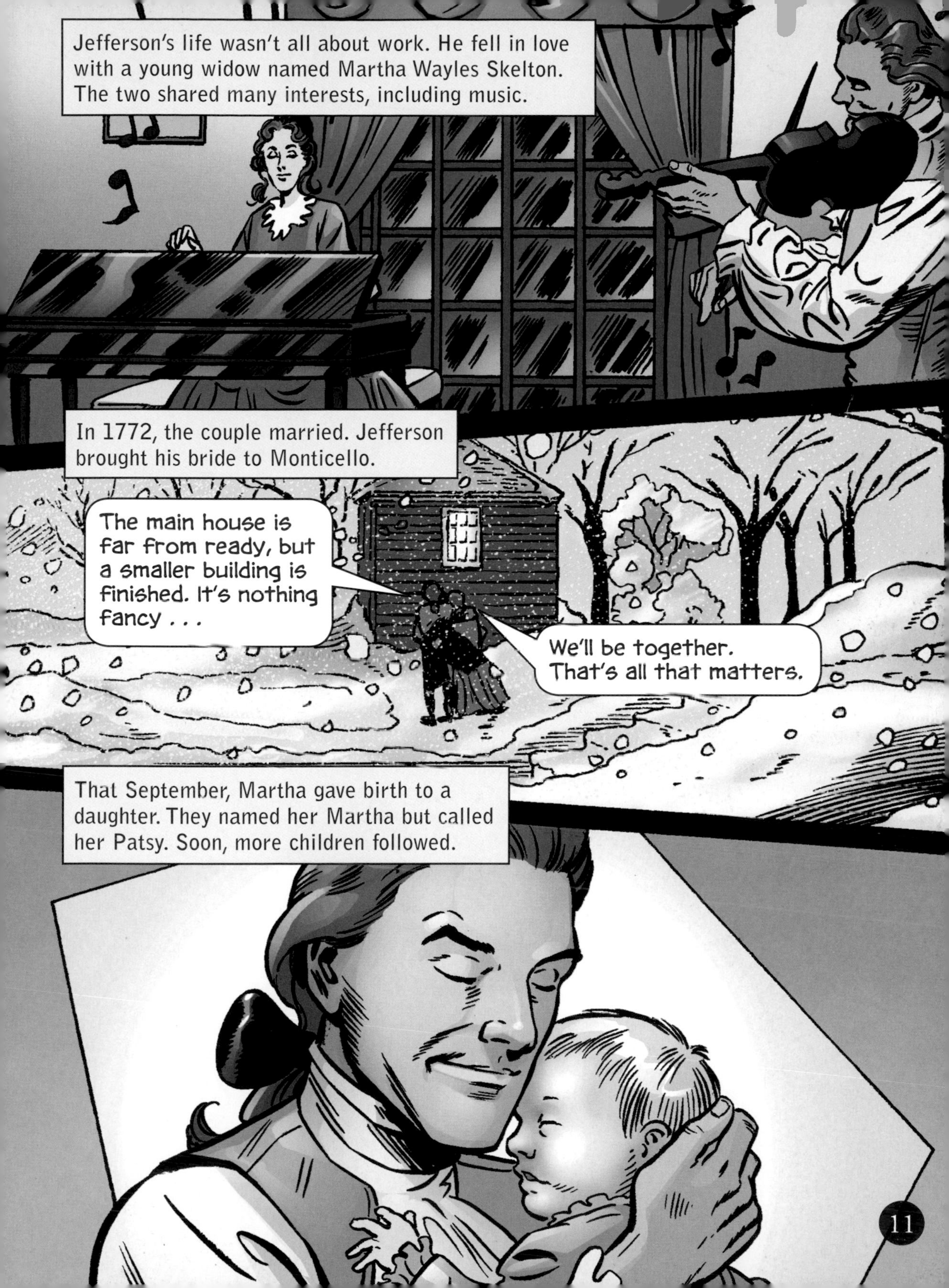
Jefferson's life wasn't all about work. He fell in love with a young widow named Martha Wayles Skelton. The two shared many interests, including music.
In 1772, the couple married. Jefferson brought his bride to Monticello.
The main house is far from ready, but a smaller building is finished. It's nothing fancy . . .
We'll be together. That's all that matters.
That September, Martha gave birth to a daughter. They named her Martha but called her Patsy. Soon, more children followed.

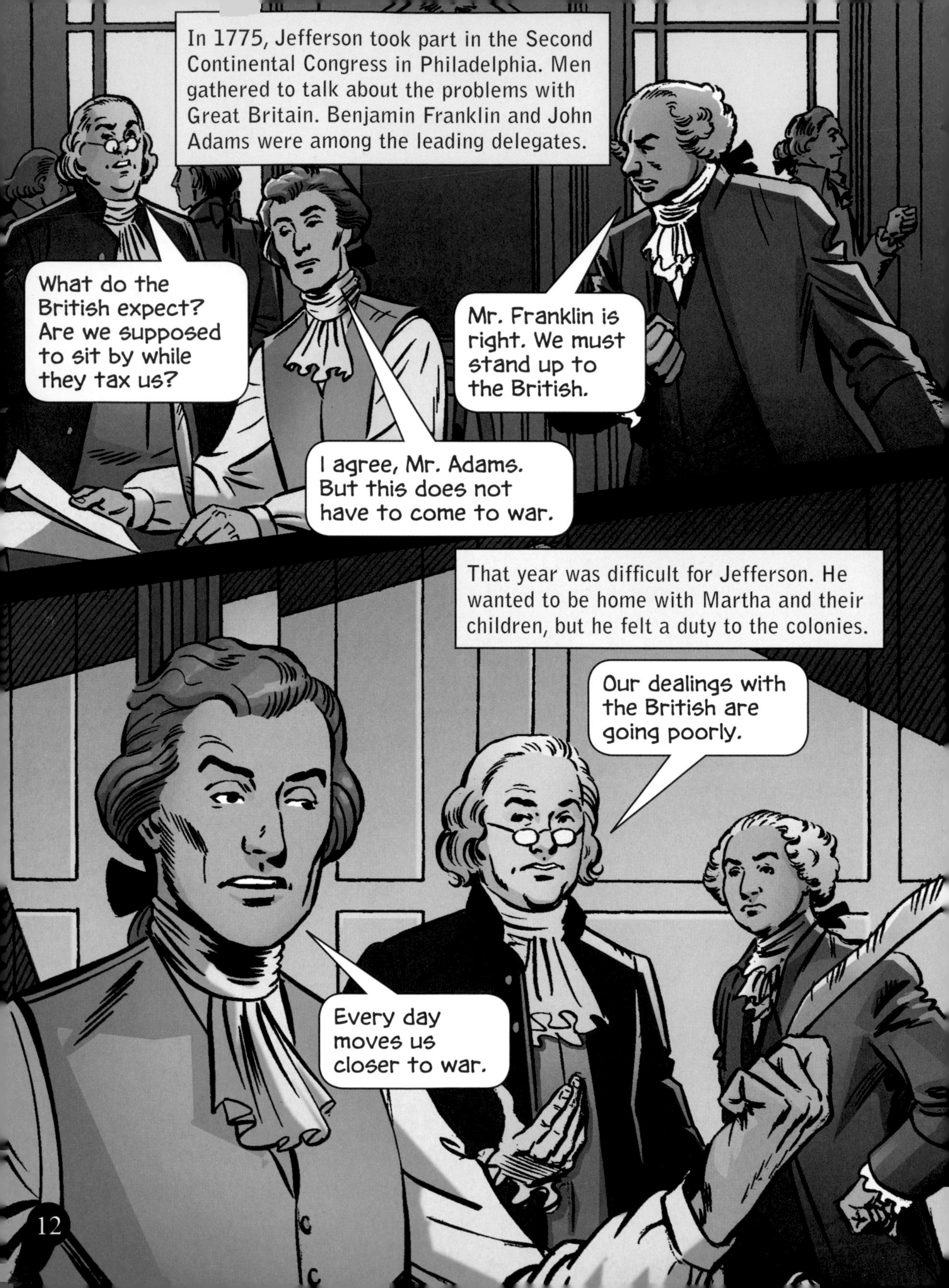
In 1775, Jefferson took part in the Second Continental Congress in Philadelphia. Men gathered to talk about the problems with Great Britain. Benjamin Franklin and John Adams were among the leading delegates.
What do the British expect? Are we supposed to sit by while they tax us?
Mr. Franklin is right. We must stand up to the British.
I agree, Mr. Adams. But this does not have to come to war.
That year was difficult for Jefferson. He wanted to be home with Martha and their children, but he felt a duty to the colonies.
Our dealings with the British are going poorly.
Every day moves us closer to war.

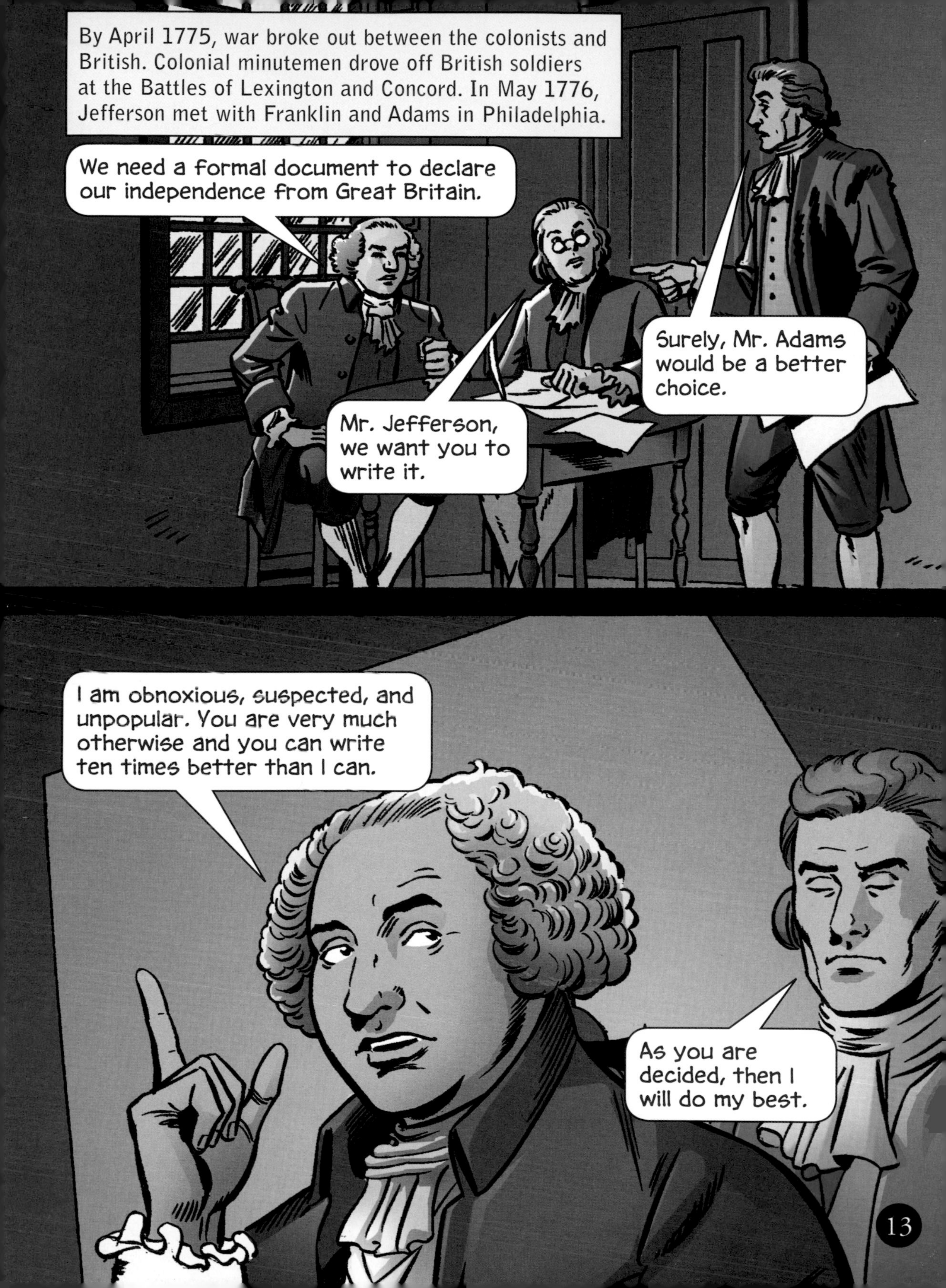
By April 1775, war broke out between the colonists and British. Colonial minutemen drove off British soldiers at the Battles of Lexington and Concord. In May 1776, Jefferson met with Franklin and Adams in Philadelphia.
We need a formal document to declare our independence from Great Britain.
Mr. Jefferson, we want you to write it.
Surely, Mr. Adams would be a better choice.
I am obnoxious, suspected, and unpopular. You are very much otherwise and you can write ten times better than I can.
As you are decided, then I will do my best.

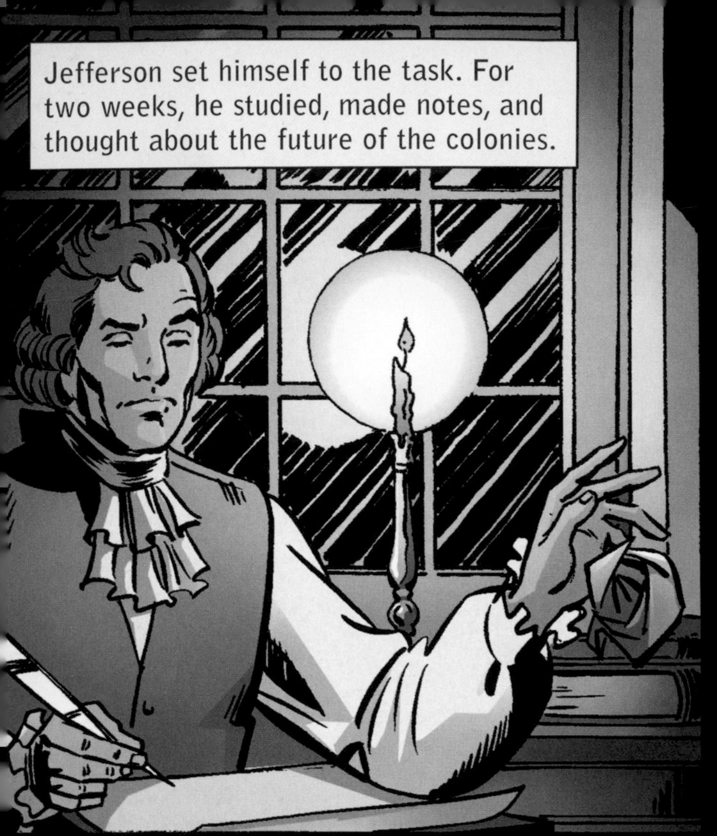
Jefferson set himself to the task. For two weeks, he studied, made notes, and thought about the future of the colonies.

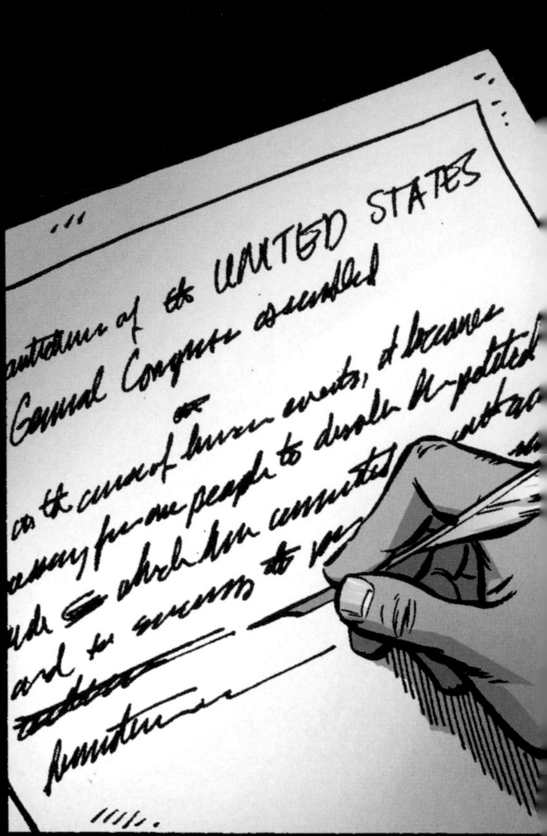
UNITED STATES

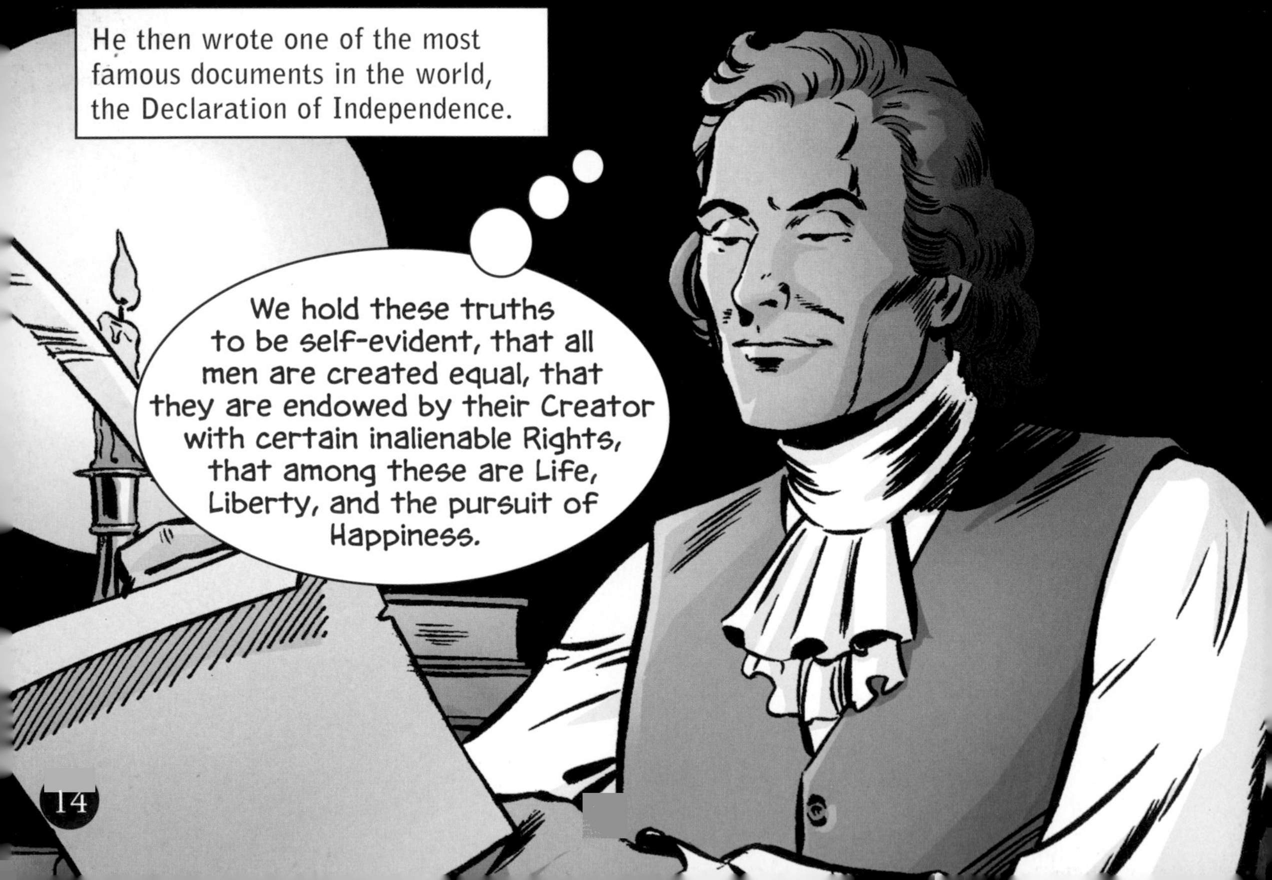
He then wrote one of the most famous documents in the world, the Declaration of Independence.
We hold these truths to be self-evident, that all men are created equal, that they are endowed by their Creator with certain inalienable Rights, that among these are Life, Liberty, and the pursuit of Happiness.

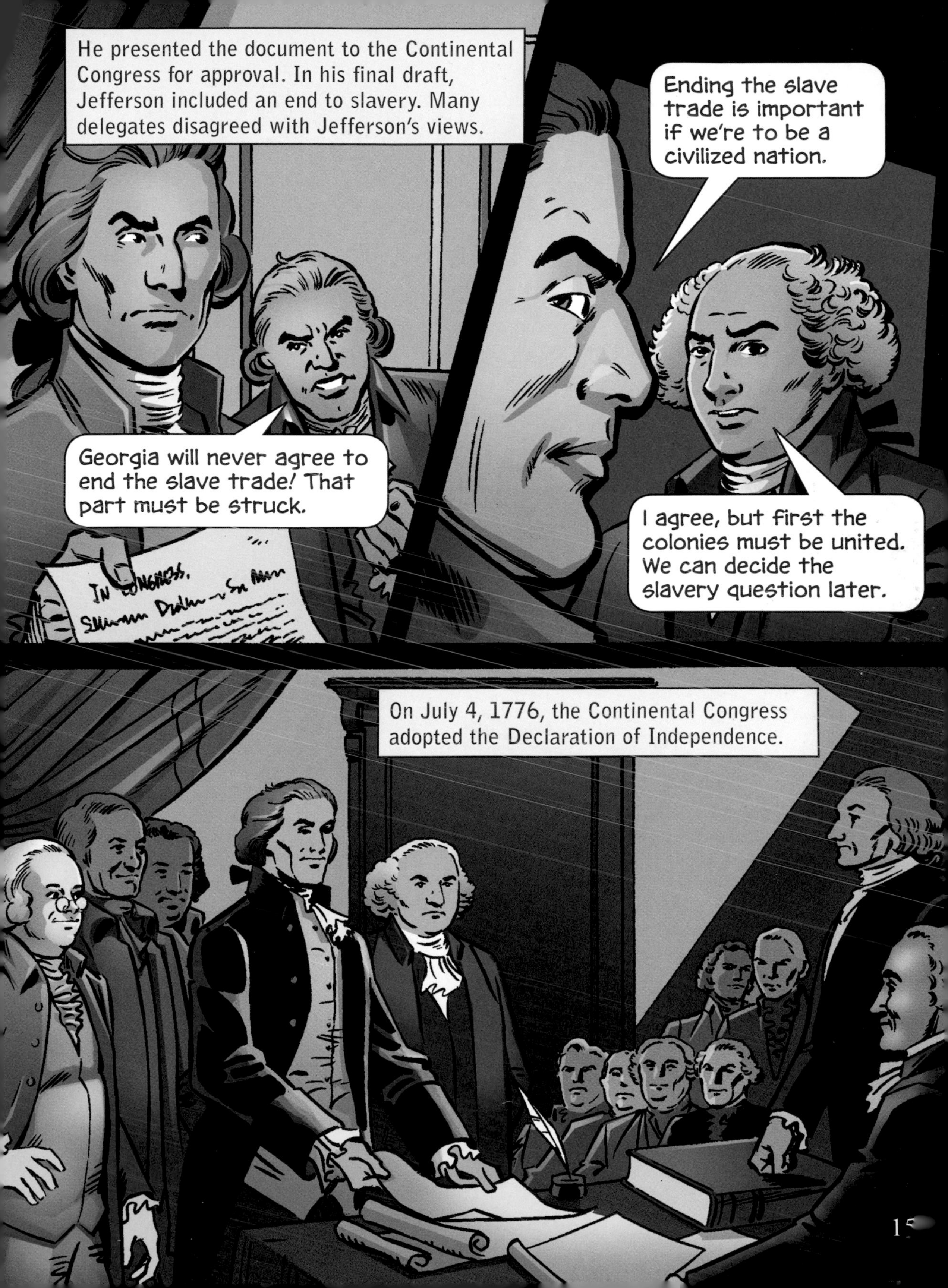
He presented the document to the Continental Congress for approval. In his final draft, Jefferson included an end to slavery. Many delegates disagreed with Jefferson's views.
Georgia will never agree to end the slave trade! That part must be struck.
Ending the slave trade is important if we're to be a civilized nation.
I agree, but first the colonies must be united. We can decide the slavery question later.
On July 4, 1776, the Continental Congress adopted the Declaration of Independence.

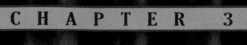

TRIUMPH and TRAGEDY

In 1779, at age 36, Jefferson was elected governor of Virginia. But soon, British troops invaded the area around Charlottesville, Virginia. After sending his family to safety, Jefferson watched in hiding as British troops took over his home.

We're looking for Governor Jefferson. Tell us where he is.

No. Not my home. How dare the British take over Monticello?!

I do not know, sir.

With the help of France, the war turned in the colonists' favor. In 1781, the British were defeated in Virginia. The colonists won the war and independence.

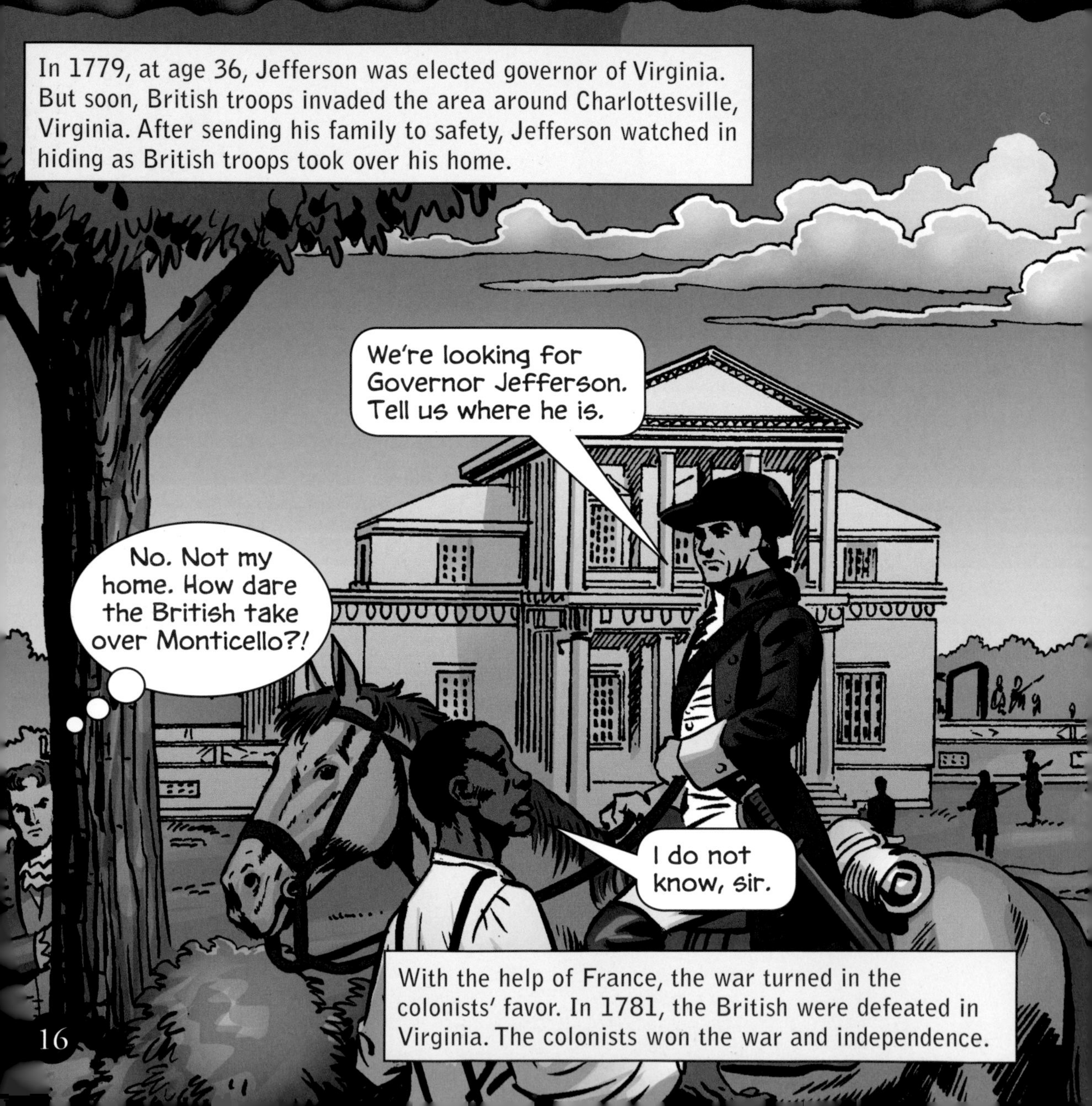

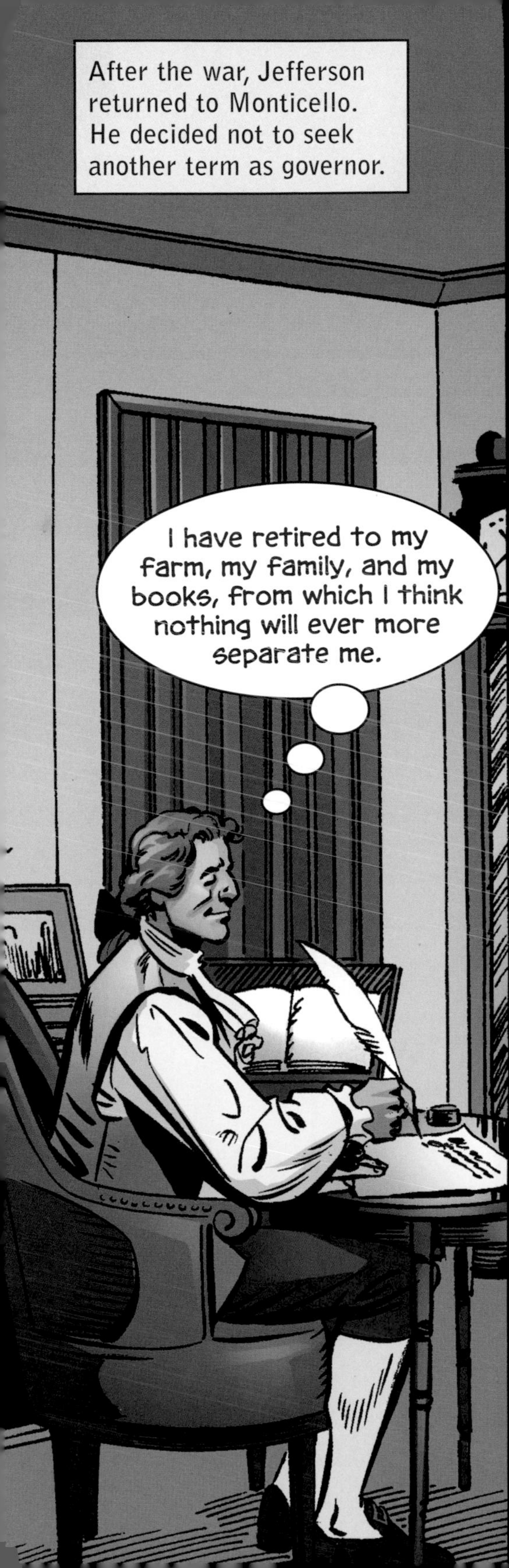
After the war, Jefferson returned to Monticello. He decided not to seek another term as governor.
I have retired to my farm, my family, and my books, from which I think nothing will ever more separate me.

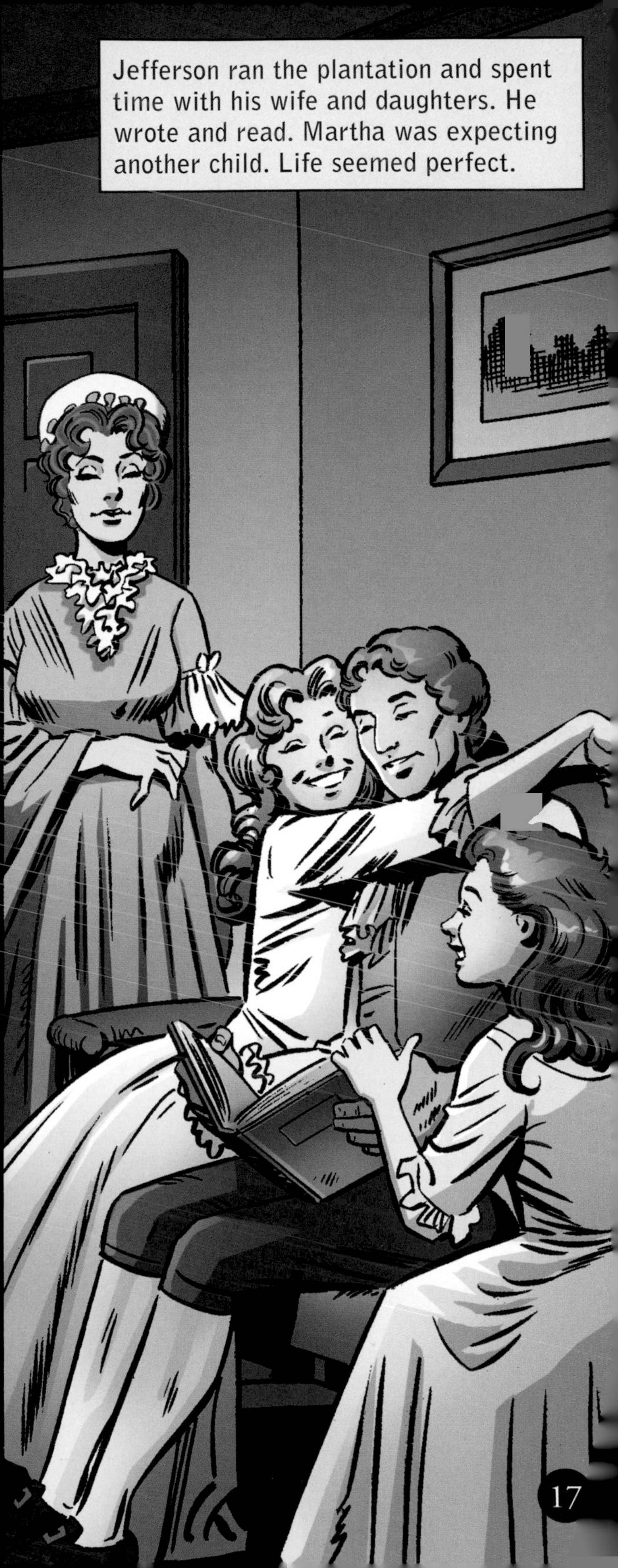
Jefferson ran the plantation and spent time with his wife and daughters. He wrote and read. Martha was expecting another child. Life seemed perfect.

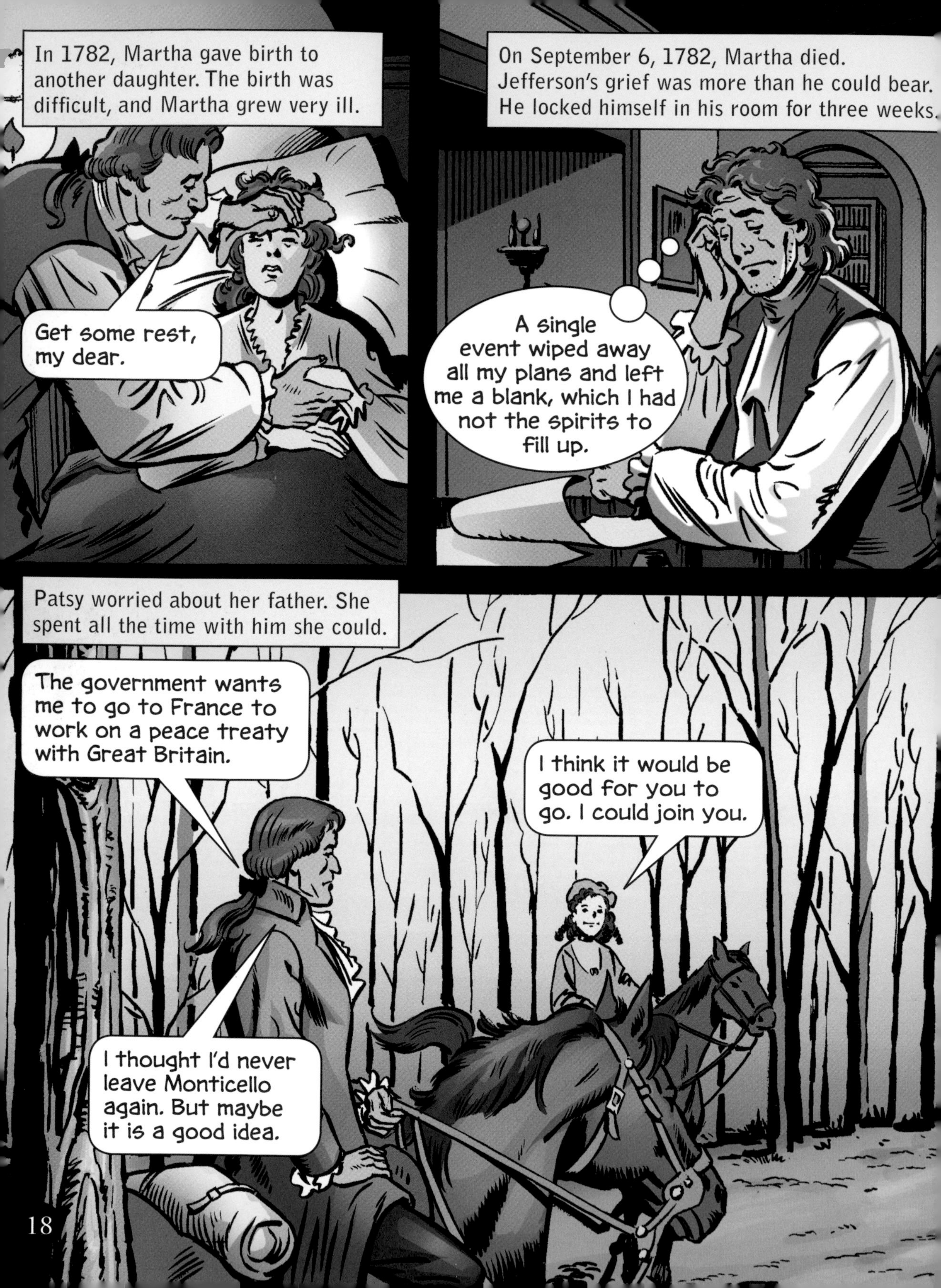
In 1782, Martha gave birth to another daughter. The birth was difficult, and Martha grew very ill.
Get some rest, my dear.
On September 6, 1782, Martha died. Jefferson's grief was more than he could bear. He locked himself in his room for three weeks.
A single event wiped away all my plans and left me a blank, which I had not the spirits to fill up.
Patsy worried about her father. She spent all the time with him she could.
The government wants me to go to France to work on a peace treaty with Great Britain.
I think it would be good for you to go. I could join you.
I thought I'd never leave Monticello again. But maybe it is a good idea.

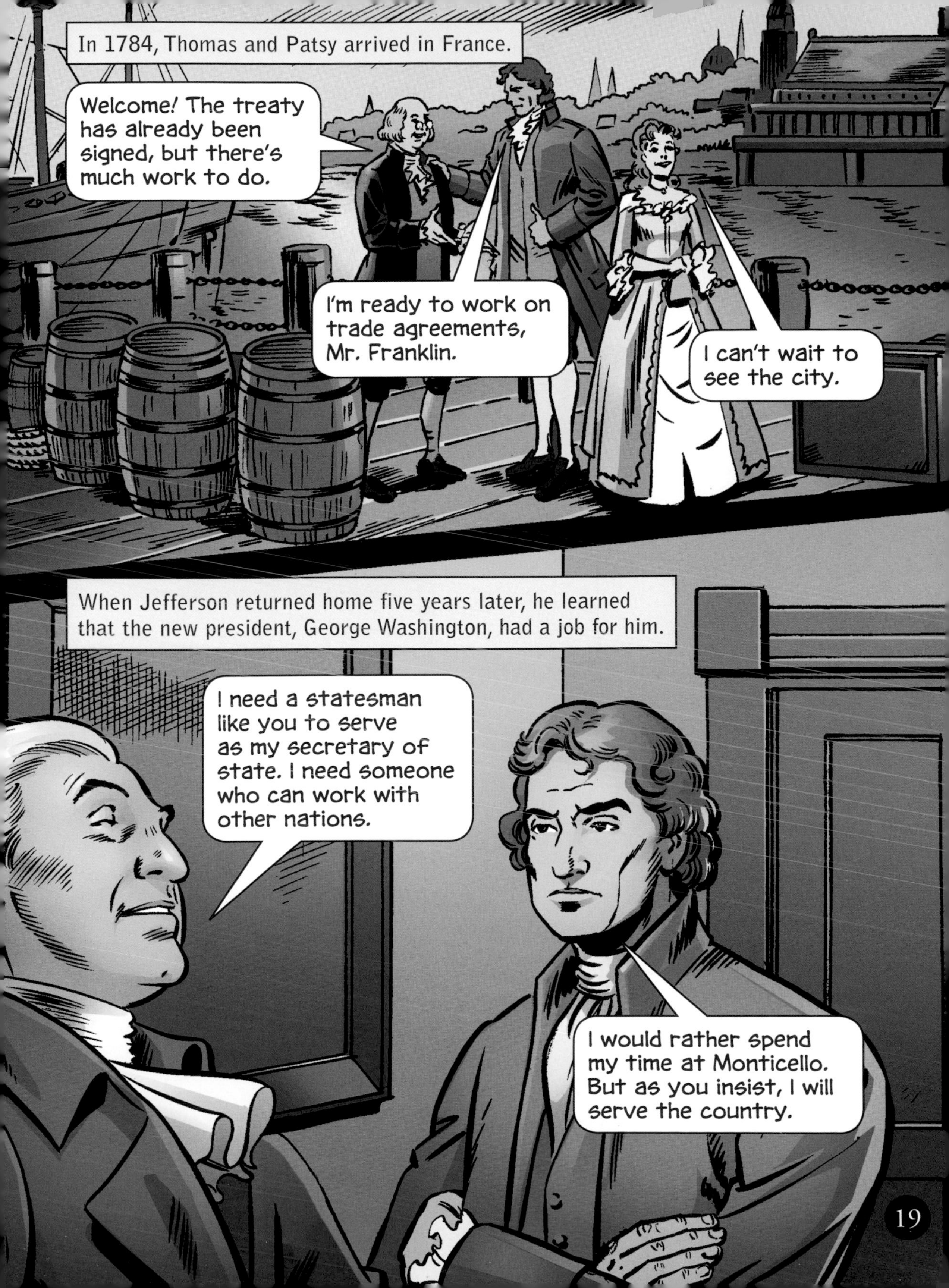
In 1784, Thomas and Patsy arrived in France.
Welcome! The treaty has already been signed, but there's much work to do.
I'm ready to work on trade agreements, Mr. Franklin.
I can't wait to see the city.
When Jefferson returned home five years later, he learned that the new president, George Washington, had a job for him.
I need a statesman like you to serve as my secretary of state. I need someone who can work with other nations.
I would rather spend my time at Monticello. But as you insist, I will serve the country.

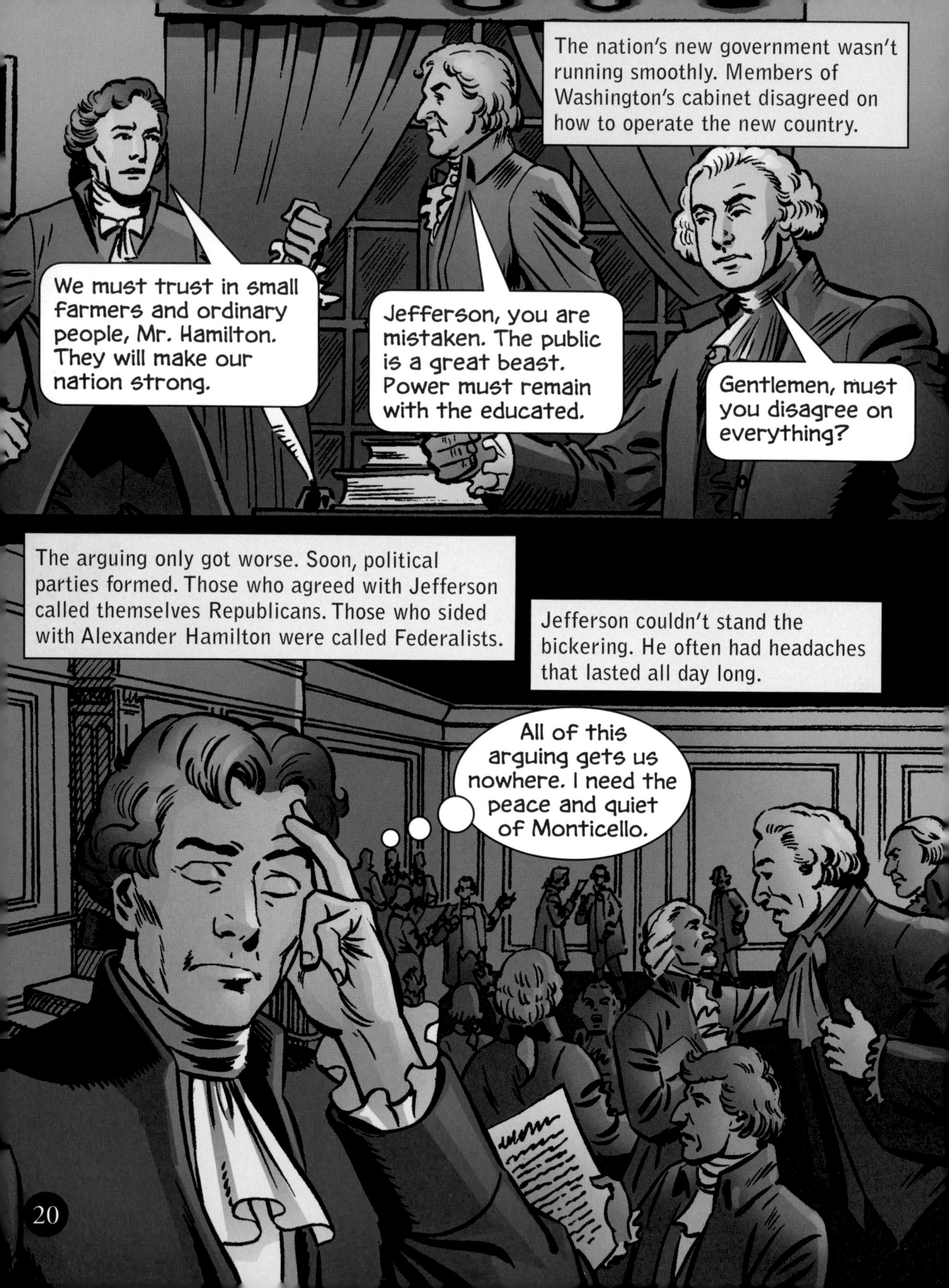
The nation's new government wasn't running smoothly. Members of Washington's cabinet disagreed on how to operate the new country.
We must trust in small farmers and ordinary people, Mr. Hamilton. They will make our nation strong.
Jefferson, you are mistaken. The public is a great beast. Power must remain with the educated.
Gentlemen, must you disagree on everything?
The arguing only got worse. Soon, political parties formed. Those who agreed with Jefferson called themselves Republicans. Those who sided with Alexander Hamilton were called Federalists.
Jefferson couldn't stand the bickering. He often had headaches that lasted all day long.
All of this arguing gets us nowhere. I need the peace and quiet of Monticello.

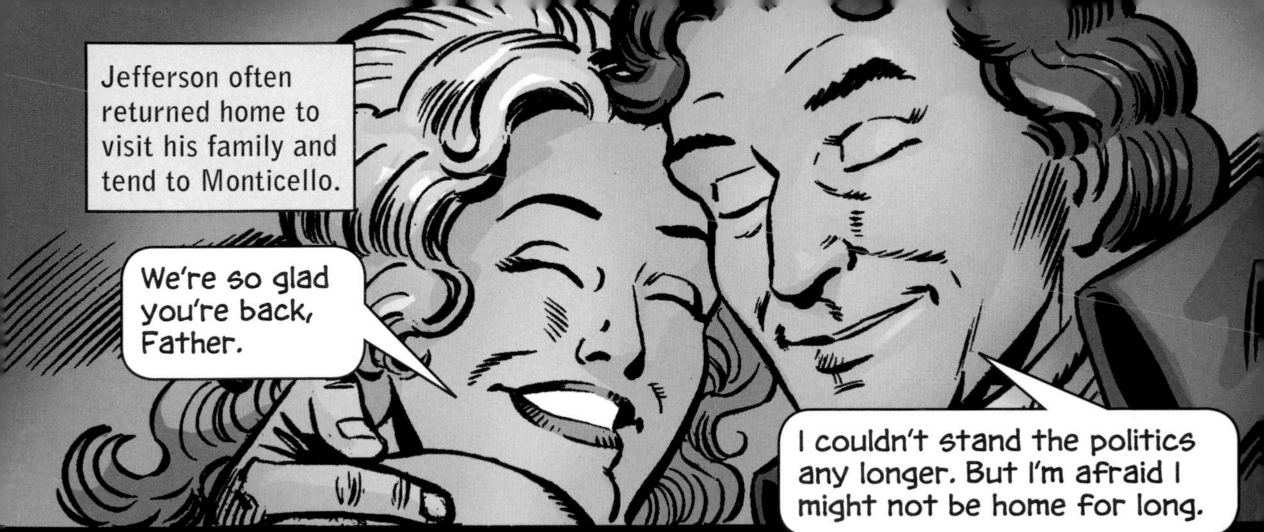
Jefferson often returned home to visit his family and tend to Monticello.
We're so glad you're back, Father.
I couldn't stand the politics any longer. But I'm afraid I might not be home for long.

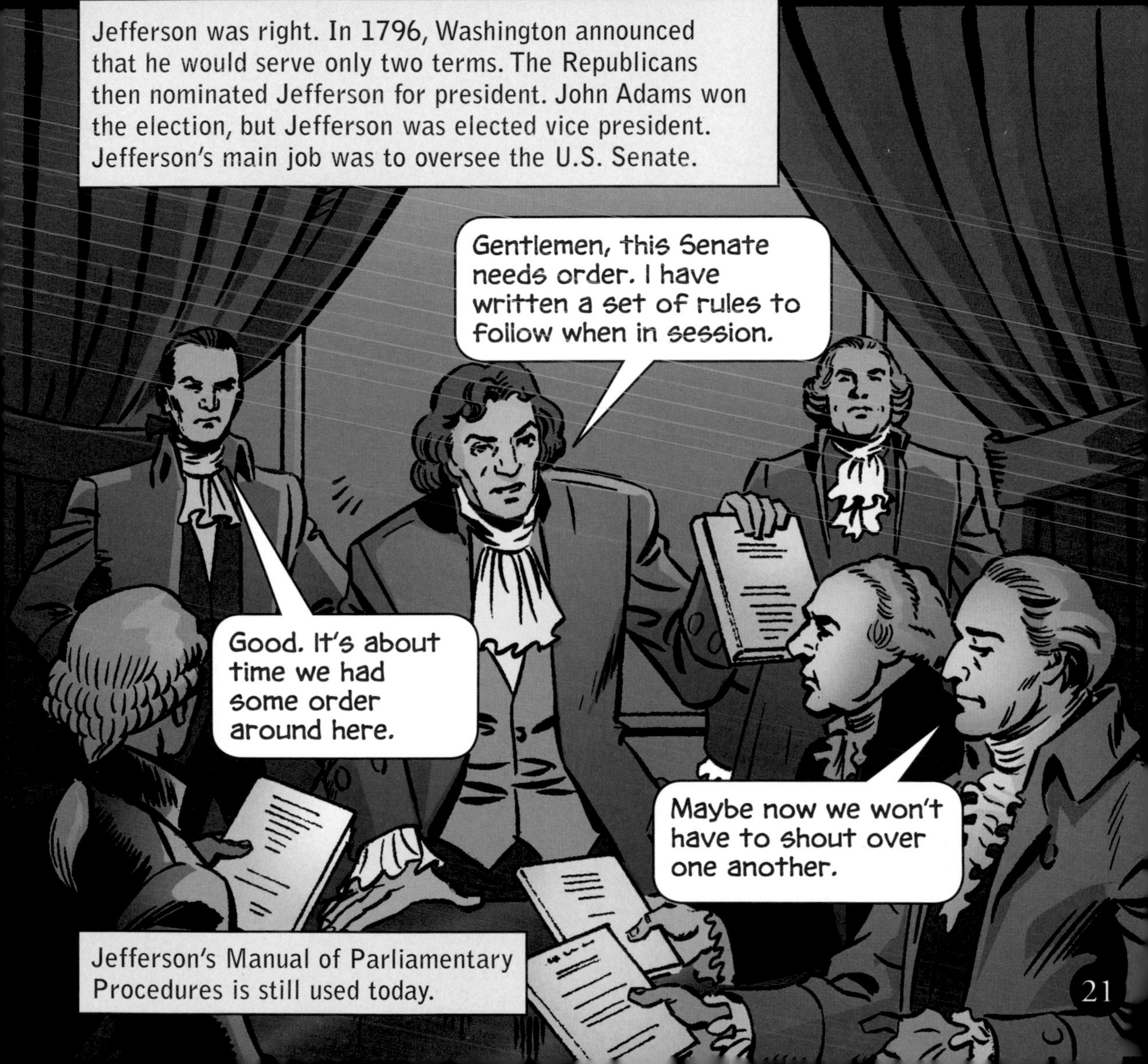
Jefferson was right. In 1796, Washington announced that he would serve only two terms. The Republicans then nominated Jefferson for president. John Adams won the election, but Jefferson was elected vice president. Jefferson's main job was to oversee the U.S. Senate.
Gentlemen, this Senate needs order. I have written a set of rules to follow when in session.
Good. It's about time we had some order around here.
Maybe now we won't have to shout over one another.
Jefferson's Manual of Parliamentary Procedures is still used today.

CHAPTER 4

PRESIDENT JEFFERSON

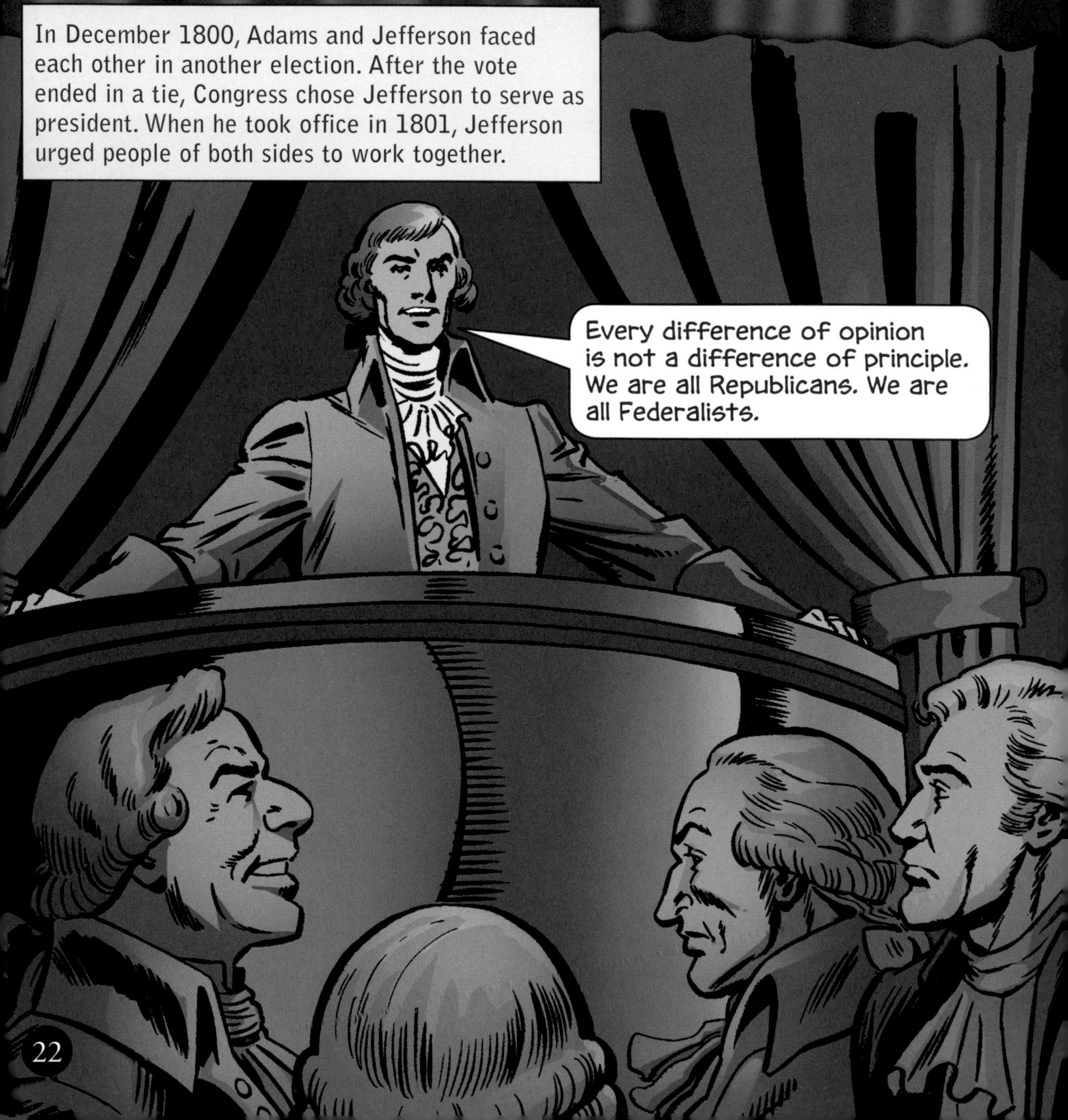
In December 1800, Adams and Jefferson faced each other in another election. After the vote ended in a tie, Congress chose Jefferson to serve as president. When he took office in 1801, Jefferson urged people of both sides to work together.
Every difference of opinion is not a difference of principle. We are all Republicans. We are all Federalists.

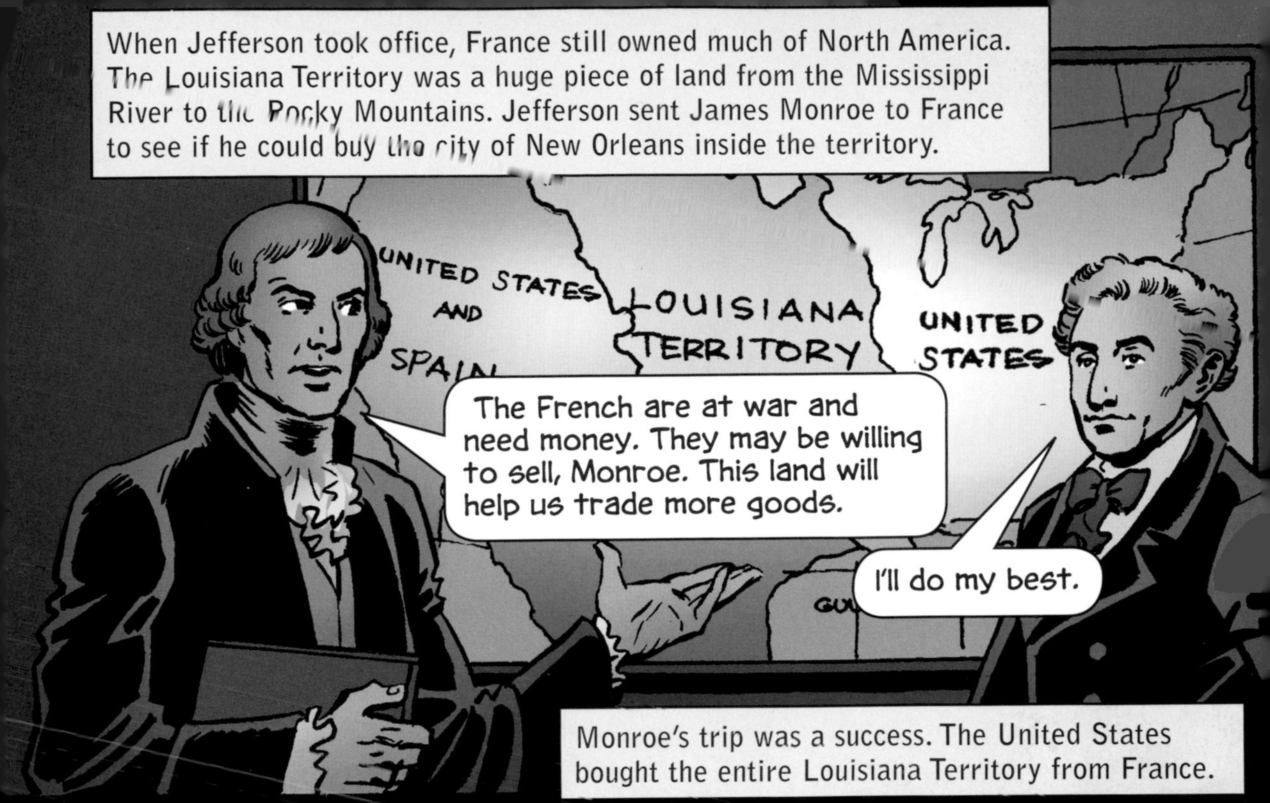
When Jefferson took office, France still owned much of North America. The Louisiana Territory was a huge piece of land from the Mississippi River to the Rocky Mountains. Jefferson sent James Monroe to France to see if he could buy the city of New Orleans inside the territory.
UNITED STATES AND SPAIN
LOUISIANA TERRITORY
UNITED STATES
The French are at war and need money. They may be willing to sell, Monroe. This land will help us trade more goods.
I'll do my best.
Monroe's trip was a success. The United States bought the entire Louisiana Territory from France.

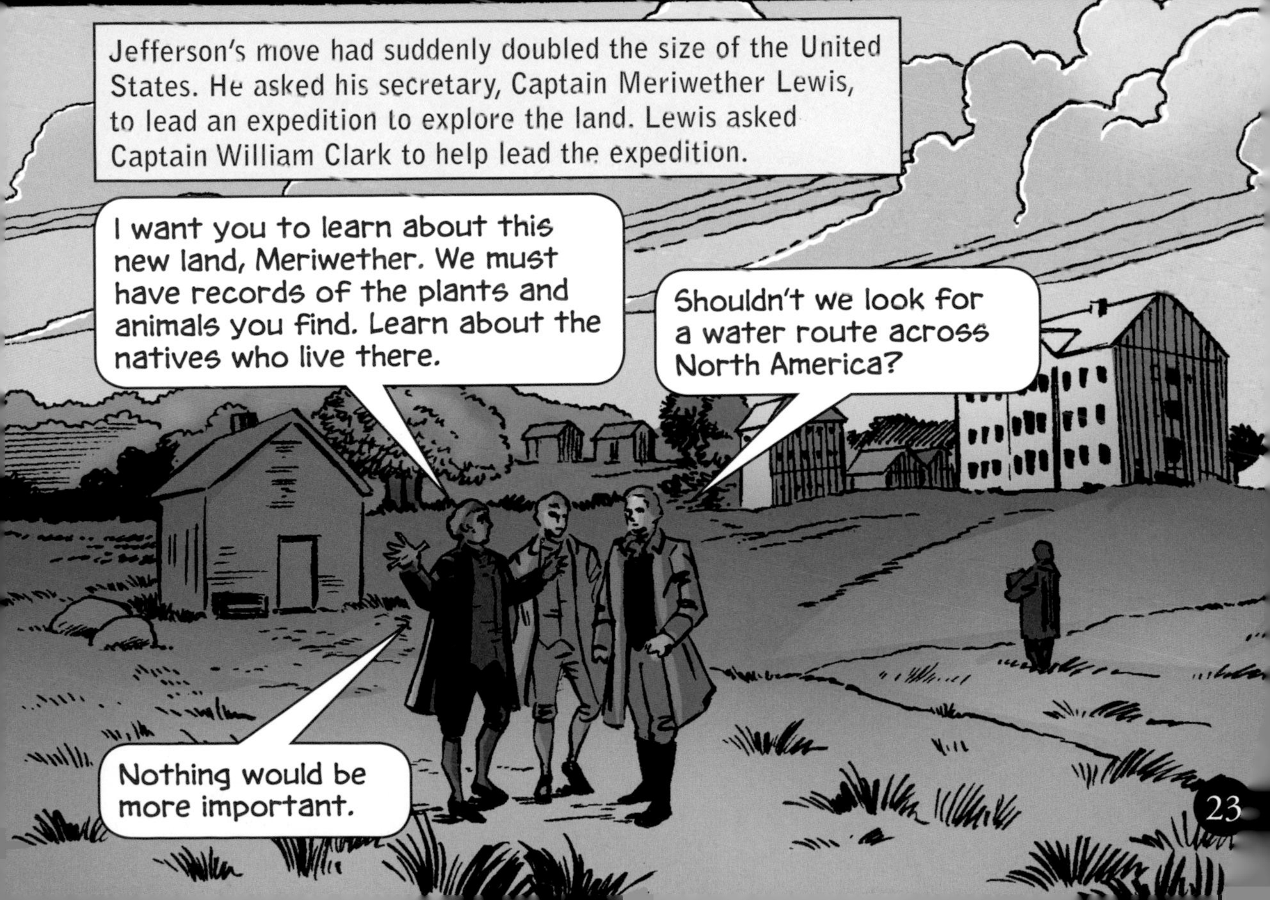
Jefferson's move had suddenly doubled the size of the United States. He asked his secretary, Captain Meriwether Lewis, to lead an expedition to explore the land. Lewis asked Captain William Clark to help lead the expedition.
I want you to learn about this new land, Meriwether. We must have records of the plants and animals you find. Learn about the natives who live there.
Shouldn't we look for a water route across North America?
Nothing would be more important.

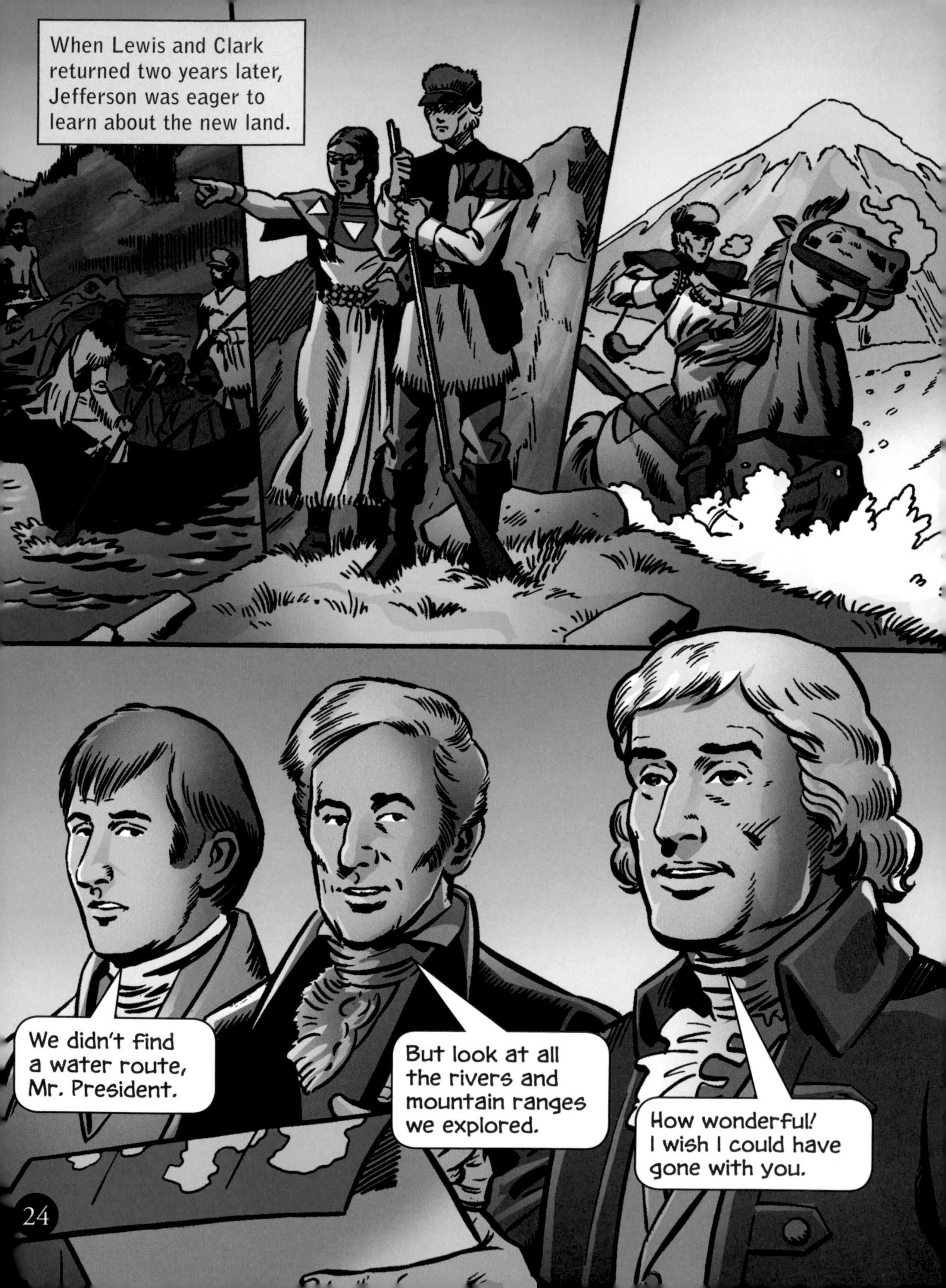

When Lewis and Clark returned two years later, Jefferson was eager to learn about the new land.
We didn't find a water route, Mr. President.
But look at all the rivers and mountain ranges we explored.
How wonderful! I wish I could have gone with you.

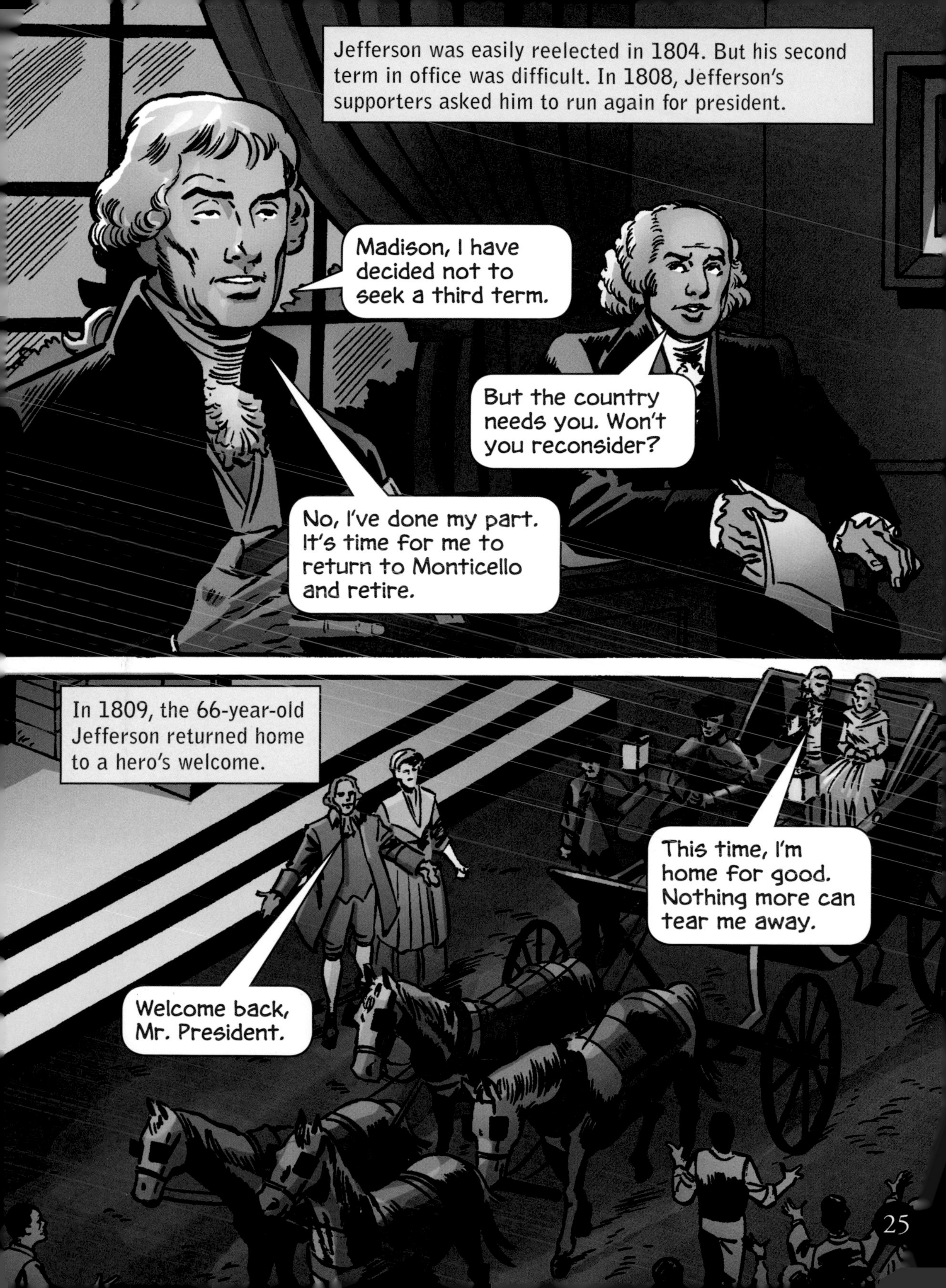
Jefferson was easily reelected in 1804. But his second term in office was difficult. In 1808, Jefferson's supporters asked him to run again for president.
Madison, I have decided not to seek a third term.
But the country needs you. Won't you reconsider?
No, I've done my part. It's time for me to return to Monticello and retire.
In 1809, the 66-year-old Jefferson returned home to a hero's welcome.
This time, I'm home for good. Nothing more can tear me away.
Welcome back, Mr. President.

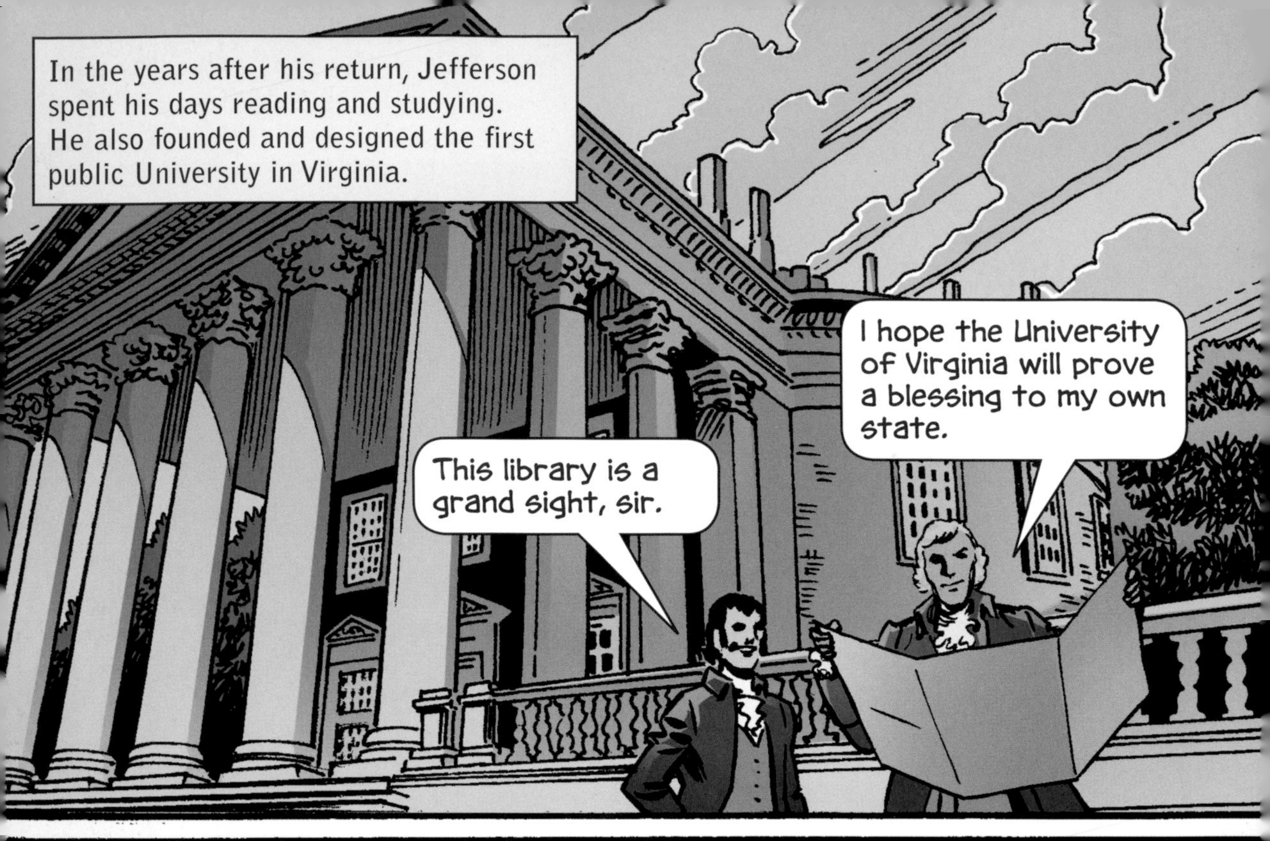
In the years after his return, Jefferson spent his days reading and studying. He also founded and designed the first public University in Virginia.
This library is a grand sight, sir.
I hope the University of Virginia will prove a blessing to my own state.

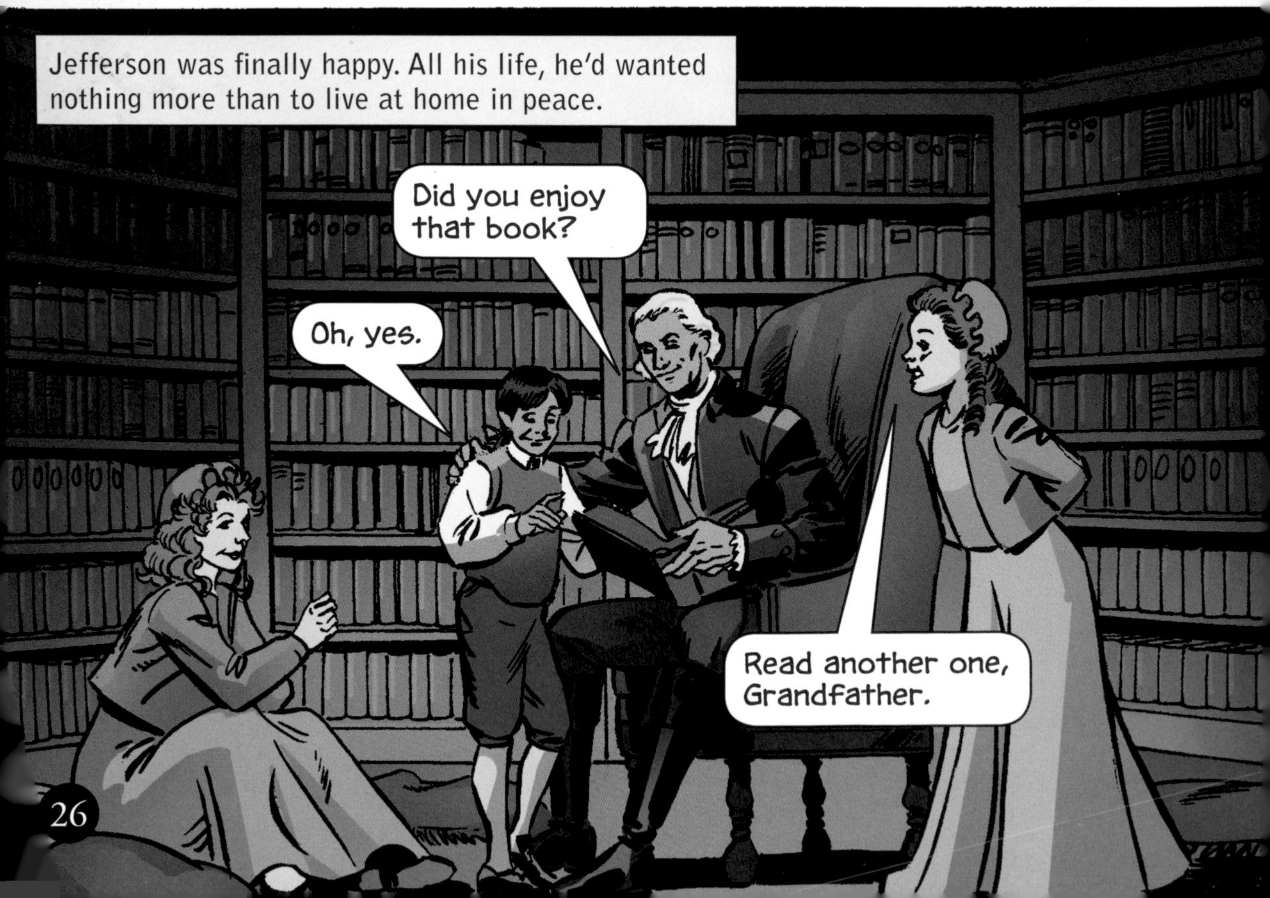
Jefferson was finally happy. All his life, he'd wanted nothing more than to live at home in peace.
Did you enjoy that book?
Oh, yes.
Read another one, Grandfather.

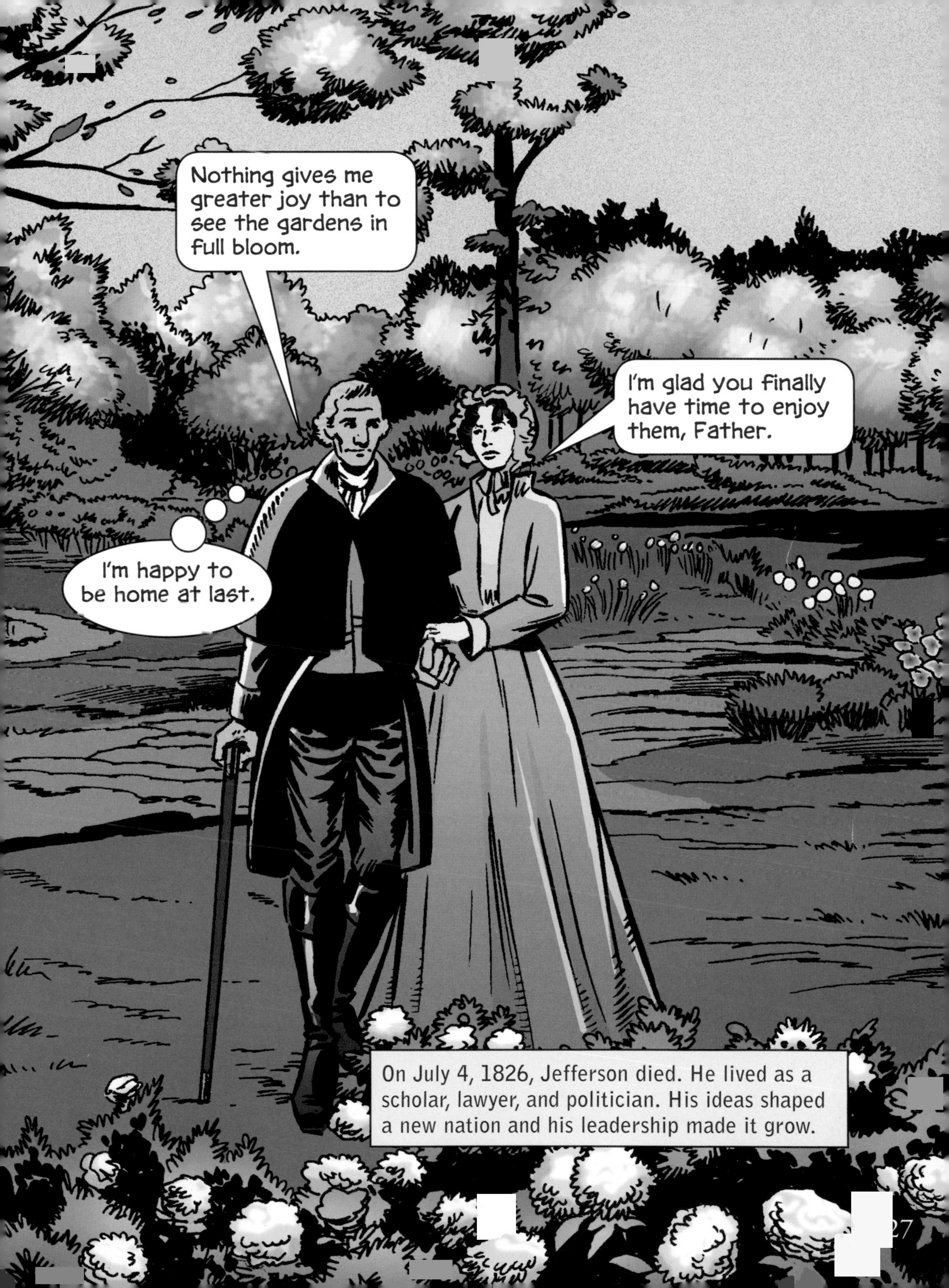
Nothing gives me greater joy than to see the gardens in full bloom.
I'm glad you finally have time to enjoy them, Father.
I'm happy to be home at last.
On July 4, 1826, Jefferson died. He lived as a scholar, lawyer, and politician. His ideas shaped a new nation and his leadership made it grow.

THOMAS JEFFERSON

Thomas Jefferson was born April 13, 1743, at his family's plantation in Albemarle County, Virginia. He died at Monticello on July 4, 1826.

In 1776, Congress asked five men to form a statement about the colonies' need for independence. The Committee of Five included Jefferson, John Adams, Benjamin Franklin, Roger Sherman, and Robert Livingston. Jefferson wrote the Declaration of Independence, but committee members reviewed his work and suggested changes.

As president, Jefferson did not uphold some formal traditions of the office. Other presidents rode carriages to take the oath of office. In 1801, Jefferson simply walked up the street. As president, he often greeted guests to the White House wearing soft shoes that looked like slippers.

Originally, Jefferson planned to buy only the city of New Orleans from France. Jefferson was willing to spend $10 million to buy it. When the French agreed to sell the entire Louisiana Territory for $15 million, Jefferson was thrilled. He said it was the greatest moment of his presidency.

- In 1815, Jefferson sold 6,487 of his books to the U.S. Congress for $24,000. Today, Jefferson's books are part of the Library of Congress.
- John Adams, one of Jefferson's closest friends during the American Revolution and one of his political opponents later on, also died on July 4, 1826. When Adams died, he said, "Thomas Jefferson still survives." Adams had no way of knowing that Jefferson had died that same day.
- The Jefferson Memorial was completed in 1943. Located in the East Potomac Park in Washington, D.C., the monument is designed in a Roman style with tall columns. The style of the monument is a tribute to Jefferson's love of classical architecture.
- Today, Monticello is a popular tourist spot. After changing hands several times after Jefferson's death, the estate finally was sold to the Thomas Jefferson Foundation in 1923. The foundation restored the buildings and opened them for public viewing.

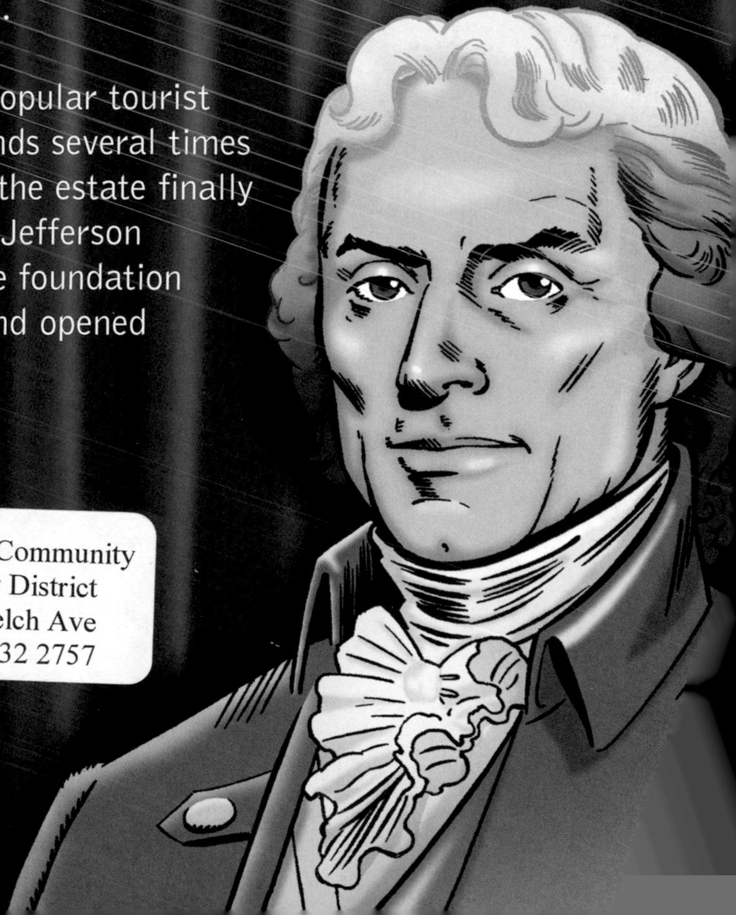

Glossary

architecture (AR-ki-tek-chur)—the activity of designing buildings

cabinet (KAB-in-it)—a group of advisors who help the president

colony (KOL-uh-nee)—a territory that has been settled by people from another country and is controlled by that country

plantation (plan-TAY-shuhn)—a large farm where crops such as tobacco and cotton are grown

tobacco (tuh-BAK-oh)—a plant with large leaves that are ground up for smoking

treaty (TREE-tee)—a formal agreement between countries

Internet Sites

FactHound offers a safe, fun way to find Internet sites related to this book. All of the sites on FactHound have been researched by our staff.

Here's how:

1. *Visit www.facthound.com*
2. Type in this special code **0736854886** for age-appropriate sites. Or enter a search word related to this book for a more general search.
3. Click on the **Fetch It** button.

FactHound will fetch the best sites for you!

Read More

Armentrout, David, and Patricia Armentrout. *The Declaration of Independence.* Documents That Shaped the Nation. Vero Beach, Fla.: Rourke, 2005.

Behrman, Carol H. *Thomas Jefferson.* Just the Facts Biographies. Minneapolis: Lerner, 2006.

Burgan, Michael. *Monticello.* We the People. Minneapolis: Compass Point, 2004.

Sherrow, Victoria. *Thomas Jefferson.* History Maker Bios. Minneapolis: Lerner, 2002.

Bibliography

Cunningham, Noble E. *In Pursuit of Reason: The Life of Thomas Jefferson.* Baton Rouge, La.: Louisiana State University Press, 1987.

Malone, Dumas. *Jefferson and His Time.* Boston: Little, Brown, 1948.

Mapp, Alf J. *Thomas Jefferson: Passionate Pilgrim: The Presidency, the Founding of the University, and the Private Battle.* Lanham, Md.: Madison Books, 1991.

Index

13 colonies, 4, 9, 10, 12, 14, 15, 28

Adams, John, 12, 13, 15, 21, 22, 28, 29

Carr, Dabney, 6
Clark, William, 23, 24

Declaration of Independence, 14–15, 28

Franklin, Benjamin, 12, 13, 19, 28

House of Burgesses, 10
Howell, Samuel, 9

Jefferson, Jane (mother), 5
Jefferson, Martha "Patsy" (daughter), 11, 18, 19, 21, 27
Jefferson, Peter (father), 4–5
Jefferson, Thomas
  birth of, 28
  children of, 11, 12, 17, 18, 19, 21
  death of, 27, 28
  education of, 5, 6, 7
  as lawyer, 7, 8, 9

  as president, 22–25, 28
  writes Declaration, 13, 14, 28

Lewis, Meriwether, 23, 24
Louisiana Purchase, 23, 28

Manual of Parliamentary Procedures, 21
Monticello, 8, 11, 16, 17, 18, 19, 20, 21, 25, 27, 29

Revolutionary War
  start of, 13
  end of, 16

Second Continental Congress, 12, 15, 28
Shadwell, 4, 5, 6, 7, 8, 28
Skelton, Martha Wayles (wife), 11, 12, 17, 18
slavery, 5, 9, 10, 15
Small, William, 6, 7

University of Virginia, 26

Washington, George, 19, 20, 21
Wythe, George, 7